TIMED READINGS PLUS

25 Two-Part Lessons
with Questions for
Building Reading Speed and Comprehension

BOOK TEN

Edward Spargo

JAMESTOWN PUBLISHERS

a division of NTC/CONTEMPORARY PUBLISHING GROUP
Lincolnwood, Illinois USA

Timed Readings Plus, Book Ten, Level M

Selection text adapted from Compton's Encyclopedia.
Used with permission of Compton's Learning Company.

ISBN: 0-89061-912-3

Published by Jamestown Publishers,
a division of NTC/Contemporary Publishing Group, Inc.,
4255 West Touhy Avenue,
Lincolnwood, Illinois, 60646 U.S.A.

5 6 7 8 9 10 11 12   MAL   15 14 13 12 11

CONTENTS

To the Instructor

Overview

Timed Readings Plus is designed to develop both reading speed and comprehension. A timed selection in each lesson focuses on improving reading rate. A nontimed selection—the "plus" selection—follows the timed selection. The nontimed selection concentrates on building mastery in critical areas of comprehension.

The 10 books in the series span reading levels 4–13, with one book at each level. Readability of the selections was assessed by using the Fry Readability Scale. Each book contains 25 lessons; each lesson is divided into Parts A and B.

Part A includes the timed selection followed by 10 multiple-choice questions: 5 fact questions and 5 thought questions. The timed selection is 400 words long and contains subject matter that is factual, nonfiction, and textbook-like. Because everyone—regardless of level—reads a 400-word passage, the steps for the timed selection can be concurrent for everyone.

Part B includes the nontimed selection, which is more narrative than the timed selection. The length of the selection varies depending on the subject matter, which relates to the content of the timed selection. The nontimed selection is followed by five comprehension questions that address the following major comprehension skills: recognizing words in context, distinguishing fact from opinion, keeping events in order, making correct inferences, and understanding main ideas.

Getting Started

Begin by assigning students to a level. A student should start with a book that is one level below his or her current reading level. If a student's reading level is not known, a suitable starting point would be one or two levels below the student's present grade in school.

Teaching a Lesson: Part A

Work in each lesson begins with the timed selection in Part A. If you wish to have all the students in the class read a selection at the same time, you can coordinate the timing using the following method. Give students the signal to preview. Allow 15 seconds for this. Have students begin reading the selection at the same time. After one minute has passed, write on the chalkboard the time that has elapsed. Update the time at 10-second intervals (1:00, 1:10, 1:20, etc.). Tell students to copy down the last time shown on the chalkboard when they finish reading. They should then record this reading time in the space designated after the selection.

If students keep track of their own reading times, have them write the times at which they start and finish reading on a separate piece of paper and then figure and record their reading time as above.

Students should now answer the ten questions that follow the Part A selection. Responses are recorded by putting an X in the box next to the student's choice of answer. Correct responses to eight or more questions indicates satisfactory comprehension and recall.

Teaching a Lesson: Part B

When students have finished Part A, they can move on to read the Part B selection. Although brief, these selections deliver all the content needed to attack the range of comprehension questions that follow.

Students next answer the comprehension questions that follow the Part B selection. Directions for answering the questions are provided with each question. Correct responses require deliberation and discrimination.

Correcting and Scoring Answers

Using the Answer Key at the back of the book, students self-score their responses to the questions in Parts A and B. Incorrect answers should be circled and the correct answers should be marked. The number of correct answers for Part A and for Part B and the total correct answers should be tallied on the final page of the lesson.

Using the Graphs

Reading times are plotted on the Reading Rate graph at the back of the book. The legend on the graph automatically converts reading times to words-per-minute rates. Comprehension totals are plotted on the Comprehension Scores graph. Plotting automatically converts the raw scores to a comprehension percentage based on four points per correct answer.

Diagnosis and Evaluation

The Comprehension Skills Profile graph at the back of the book tracks student responses to the Part B comprehension questions. For each incorrect response, students should mark an X in the corresponding box on the graph. A column of Xs rising above other columns indicates a specific comprehension weakness. Using the profile, you can assess trends in student performance and suggest remedial work if necessary.

A student who has reached a peak in reading speed (with satisfactory comprehension) is ready to advance to the next book in the series. Before moving on to the next book, students should be encouraged to maintain their speed and comprehension on a number of lessons in order to consolidate their achievement.

HOW TO USE THIS BOOK

Getting Started

Study Part A: Reading Faster and Better. Read and learn the steps to follow and the techniques to use to help you read more quickly and more efficiently.

Study Part B: Mastering Reading Comprehension. Learn what the five categories of comprehension are all about. Knowing what kind of comprehension response is expected from you and how to achieve that response will help you better comprehend all you read.

Working a Lesson

Find the Starting Lesson. Locate the timed selection in Part A of the lesson that you are going to read. Wait for your instructor's signal to preview the selection. Your instructor will allow you 15 seconds for previewing.

Read the Part A Selection. When your instructor gives you the signal, begin reading. Read at a faster-than-normal speed. Read carefully so that you will be able to answer questions about what you have read.

Record Your Reading Time. When you finish reading, look at the blackboard and note your reading time. Write this time at the bottom of the page on the line labeled Reading Time.

Answer the Part A Questions. Answer the 10 questions that follow the selection. There are 5 fact questions and 5 thought questions. Choose the best answer to each question and put an X in that box.

Read the Part B Selection. This passage is less textbook-like and more story-like than the timed selection. Read well enough so that you can answer the questions that follow.

Answer the Part B Questions. These questions are different from traditional multiple-choice questions. In answering these questions, you must make three choices for each question. Instructions for answering each category of question are given. There are 15 responses for you to record.

Correct Your Answers. Use the Answer Key at the back of the book. For the Part A questions, circle any wrong answer and put an X in the box you should have marked. For the Part B questions, circle any wrong answer and write the correct letter or number next to it.

Scoring Your Work

Total Your Correct Answers. Count your correct answers for Part A and for Part B. Record those numbers on the appropriate lines at the end of the lesson. Then add the two scores to determine your total correct answers. Record that number on the appropriate line.

Plotting Your Progress

Plot Your Reading Time. Refer to the Reading Rate graph on page 116. On the vertical line that represents your lesson, put an X at the point where it intersects your reading time, shown along the left-hand side. The right-hand side of the graph will reveal your words-per-minute reading speed. Your instructor will review this graph from time to time to evaluate your progress.

Plot Your Comprehension Scores. Record your comprehension scores on the graph on page 117. On the vertical line that represents your lesson, put an X at the point where it intersects your total correct answers, shown along the left-hand side. The right-hand side of the graph will reveal your comprehension percentage. Your instructor will want to review this graph, too. Your achievement, as shown on both graphs, will determine your readiness to move on to higher and more challenging levels.

Plot Your Comprehension Skills. You will find the Comprehension Skills Profile on page 118. It is used to record your wrong answers only for the Part B questions. The five categories of questions are listed along the bottom. There are five columns of boxes, one column for each question. For every wrong answer, put an X in a box for that question. Your instructor will use this graph to detect any comprehension problems you may be experiencing.

PART A: READING FASTER AND BETTER

Step 1: Preview

When you read, do you start in with the first word, or do you look over the whole selection for a moment? Good readers preview the selection first. This helps make them good—and fast—readers. Here are the steps to follow when previewing the timed selection in Part A of each unit.

1. Read the Title. Titles are designed not only to announce the subject, but also to make the reader think. What can you learn from the title? What thoughts does it bring to mind? What do you already know about this subject?

2. Read the First Sentence. Read the first two sentences if they are short. The opening sentence is the writer's opportunity to greet the reader. Some writers announce what they hope to tell you in the selection. Some writers tell you why they are writing. Other writers just try to get your attention.

3. Read the Last Sentence. Read the final two sentences if they are short. The closing sentence is the writer's last chance to talk to you. Some writers repeat the main idea once more. Some writers draw a conclusion—this is what they have been leading up to. Other writers summarize their thoughts; they tie all the facts together.

4. Scan the Selection. Glance through the selection quickly to see what else you can pick up. Look for anything that can help you read the selection. Are there names, dates, or numbers? If so, you may have to read more slowly. Is the selection informative—containing a lot of facts, or is it conversational—an informal discussion with the reader?

Step 2: Read for Meaning

When you read, do you just see words? Are you so occupied reading words that you sometimes fail to get the meaning? Good readers see beyond the words—they seek the meaning. This makes them faster readers.

1. Build Concentration. You cannot read with understanding if you are not concentrating. When you discover that your thoughts are straying, correct the situation right away. Avoid distractions and distracting situations. Keep the preview information in mind. This will help focus your attention on the selection.

2. Read in Thought Groups. A reader should strive to see words in meaningful combinations. If you see only a word at a time (called word-by-word reading), your comprehension suffers along with your speed.

3. Question the Writer. To sustain the pace you have set for yourself, and to maintain a high level of concentration and comprehension, question the writer as you read. Ask yourself such questions as, "What does this mean? How can I use this information?"

Step 3: Grasp Paragraph Sense

The paragraph is the basic unit of meaning. If you can discover quickly and understand the main point of each paragraph, you can comprehend the writer's message. Good readers know how to find the main ideas quickly. This helps make them faster readers.

1. Find the Topic Sentence. The topic sentence, which contains the main idea, is often the first sentence of a paragraph. It is followed by sentences that support, develop, or explain the main idea. Sometimes a topic sentence comes at the end of a paragraph. When it does, the supporting details come first, building the base for the topic sentence. Some paragraphs do not have a topic sentence; all of the sentences combine to create a meaningful idea.

2. Understand Paragraph Structure. Every well-written paragraph has a purpose. The purpose may be to inform, define, explain, illustrate, and so on. The purpose should always relate to the main idea and expand on it. As you read each paragraph, see how the body of the paragraph is used to tell you more about the main idea.

Step 4: Organize Facts

When you read, do you tend to see a lot of facts without any apparent connection or relationship? Understanding how the facts all fit together to deliver the writer's message is, after all, the reason for reading. Good readers organize facts as they read. This helps them read rapidly and well.

1. Discover the Writer's Plan. Every writer has a plan or outline to follow. If you can discover the writer's method of organization, you have a key to understanding the message. Sometimes the writer gives you obvious signals. The statement, "There are three reasons . . .," should prompt you to look for a listing of the three items. Other less obvious signal words such as *moreover, otherwise,* and *consequently* tell you the direction the writer is taking in delivering a message.

2. Relate as You Read. As you read the selection, keep the information learned during the preview in mind. See how the writer is attempting to piece together a meaningful message. As you discover the relationship among the ideas, the message comes through quickly and clearly.

PART B: MASTERING READING COMPREHENSION

Recognizing Words in Context

Always check to see if the words around a new word—its context—can give you some clue to its meaning. A word generally appears in a context related to its meaning. If the words *soil* and *seeds* appear in an article about gardens, for example, you can assume they are related to the topic of gardens.

Suppose you are unsure of the meaning of the word *expired* in the following paragraph:

> Vera wanted to take a book out, but her library card had expired.
> She had to borrow mine because she didn't have time to renew hers.

You could begin to figure out the meaning of *expired* by asking yourself, "What could have happened to Vera's library card that would make her have to borrow someone else's card?" You might realize that if she had to renew her card, it must have come to an end or run out. This would lead you to conclude that the word *expired* must mean to come to an end or run out. You would be right. The context suggested the meaning to you.

Context can also affect the meaning of a word you know. The word *key,* for instance, has many meanings. There are musical keys, door keys, and keys to solving a mystery. The context in which *key* occurs will tell you which meaning is right.

Sometimes a hard word will be explained by the words that immediately follow it. The word *grave* in the following sentence might give you trouble:

> He looked grave; there wasn't a trace of a smile on his lips.

You can figure out that the second part of the sentence explains the word *grave:* "wasn't a trace of a smile" indicates a serious look, so *grave* must mean serious.

The subject of a sentence and your knowledge about that subject might also help you determine the meaning of an unknown word. Try to decide the meaning of the word *revive* in the following sentence:

> Sunshine and water will revive those drooping plants.

The sentence is about giving plants light and water. You may know that plants need light and water to be healthy. If you know that drooping plants are not healthy, you can figure out that *revive* means to bring back to health.

Distinguishing Fact from Opinion

Every day you are called upon to sort out fact and opinion. When a friend says she saw Mel Gibson's greatest movie last night, she is giving you her opinion. When she says she saw Mel Gibson's latest movie, she may be stating a fact. The fact can be proved—you can check to confirm or verify that the movie is indeed Mel Gibson's most recent film. The opinion can be disputed—ask around and others may not agree about the film's unqualified greatness. Because much of what you read and hear contains both facts and opinions, you need to be able to tell them apart. You need the skill of distinguishing fact from opinion.

Facts are statements that can be proved true. The proof must be objective and verifiable. You must be able to check for yourself to confirm a fact.

Look at the following facts. Notice that they can be checked for accuracy and confirmed. Suggested sources for verification appear in parentheses.

- In 1998 Bill Clinton was president of the United States. (Consult newspapers, news broadcasts, election results, etc.)

- Earth revolves around the sun. (Look it up in encyclopedias or astrological journals; ask knowledgeable people.)

- Dogs walk on four legs. (See for yourself.)

Opinions are statements that cannot be proved true. There is no objective evidence you can consult to check the truthfulness of an opinion. Unlike facts, opinions express personal beliefs or judgments. Opinions reveal how someone feels about a subject, not the facts about that subject. You might agree or disagree with someone's opinion, but you cannot prove it right or wrong.

Look at the following opinions. Reasons for classification as opinions appear in parentheses.

- Bill Clinton was born to be a president. (You cannot prove this by referring to birth records. There is no evidence to support this belief.)

- Intelligent life exists on other planets in our solar system. (There is no proof of this. It may be proved true some day, but for now it is just an educated guess—not a fact.)

- Dog is man's best friend. (This is not a fact; your best friend might not be a dog.)

As you read, be aware that facts and opinions are frequently mixed together. The following passage contains both facts and opinions:

> The new 2000 Cruising Yacht offers lots of real-life interior room. It features a luxurious aft cabin, not some dim "cave." The galley

comes equipped with a full-size refrigerator and freezer. And this spacious galley has room to spare. The heads (there are two) have separate showers. The fit and finish are beyond equal and the performance is responsive and outstanding.

Did you detect that the third and fifth sentences state facts and that the rest of the sentences express opinions? Both facts and opinions are useful to you as a reader. But to evaluate what you read and to read intelligently, you need to know the difference between them.

Keeping Events in Order

Writers organize details in a pattern. They present information in a certain order. Recognizing how writers organize—and understanding that organization—can help you improve your comprehension.

When details are arranged in the precise order in which they occurred, a writer is using a chronological (or time) pattern. A writer may, however, change this order. The story may "flash back" to past events that affected the present. The story may "flash forward" to show the results of present events. The writer may move back and forth between past, present, and future to help you see the importance of events.

Making Correct Inferences

Much of what you read suggests more than it says. Writers do not always state outright what they want you to know. Frequently, they omit information that underlies the statements they make. They may assume that you already know it. They may want you to make the effort to figure out the implied information. To get the most out of what you read, you must come to an understanding about unstated information. You can do this through inference. From what is stated, you make inferences about what is not.

You make many inferences every day. Imagine, for example, that you are visiting a friend's house for the first time. You see a bag of dog food. You infer (make an inference) that the family has a dog. On another day you overhear a conversation. You catch the names of two actors and the words *scene, dialogue,* and *directing*. You infer that the people are discussing a movie or play.

In these situations and others like them, you infer unstated information from what you observe or read. Readers who cannot make inferences cannot see beyond the obvious. For the careful reader, facts are just the beginning. Facts stimulate your mind to think beyond them—to make an inference about what is meant but not stated.

The following passage is about Charles Dickens. As you read it, see how many inferences you can make.

Charles Dickens visited the United States in 1867. Wherever he went, the reception was the same. The night before, crowds arrived and lined up before the door. By morning the streets were camp-grounds, with men, women, and children sitting or sleeping on blankets. Hustlers got ten times the price of a ticket. Once inside, audiences were surprised to hear their favorite Dickens characters speak with an English accent. After 76 readings Dickens boarded a ship for England. When his fellow passengers asked him to read, he said he'd rather be put in irons!

Did you notice that many inferences may be drawn from the passage? Dickens attracted huge crowds. From that fact you can infer that he was popular. His English accent surprised audiences. You can infer that many people didn't know he was English. Hustlers got high prices for tickets. This suggests that "scalping" tickets is not new. Dickens refused to read on the ship. You can infer that he was exhausted and tired of reading aloud to audiences. Those are some obvious inferences that can be made from the passage. More subtle ones can also be made; however, if you see the obvious ones, you understand how inferences are made.

Be careful about the inferences you make. One set of facts may suggest several inferences. Not all of them will be correct; some will be faulty inferences. The correct inference is supported by enough evidence to make it more likely than other inferences.

Understanding Main Ideas

The main idea tells who or what is the subject of the paragraph or passage. The main idea is the most important idea, the idea that provides purpose and direction. The rest of the paragraph or passage explains, develops, or supports the main idea. Without a main idea, there would be only a collection of unconnected thoughts. It would be like a handle and a bowl without the "idea cup," or bread and meat without the "idea sandwich."

In the following passage, the main idea is printed in italics. As you read, observe how the other sentences develop or explain the main idea.

> *Typhoon Chris hit with full fury today on the central coast of Japan.*
> Heavy rain from the storm flooded the area. High waves carried
> many homes into the sea. People now fear that the heavy rains will
> cause mudslides in the central part of the country. The number of
> people killed by the storm may climb past the 200 mark by Saturday.

In this paragraph, the main idea statement appears first. It is followed by sentences that explain, support, or give details. Sometimes the main idea appears at the end of a paragraph. Writers often construct that type of paragraph when their purpose is to persuade or convince. Readers may be more open to a new idea if the reasons for it are presented first. As you read the following paragraph, think about the overall impact of the supporting ideas. Their purpose is to convince the reader that the main idea in the last sentence should be accepted.

> Last week there was a head-on collision at Huntington and Canton streets. Just a month ago a pedestrian was struck there. Fortunately, she was only slightly injured. In the past year there have been more accidents there than at any other corner in the city. In fact, nearly 10 percent of all city accidents occur there. This intersection is dangerous, and a traffic signal should be installed there before a life is lost.

The details in the paragraph progress from least important to most important. They achieve their full effect in the main idea statement at the end.

In many cases, the main idea is not expressed in a single sentence. The reader is called upon to interpret all of the ideas expressed and decide upon a main idea. Read the following paragraph:

> The American author Jack London was once a pupil at the Cole Grammar School in Oakland, California. Each morning the class sang a song. When the teacher noticed that Jack wouldn't sing, she sent him to the principal. He returned to class with a note. It said that he could be excused from singing if he would write an essay every morning.

In this paragraph, the reader has to interpret the individual ideas and decide on a main idea. This main idea seems reasonable: Jack London's career as a writer began with a "punishment" in grammar school.

Understanding the concept of the main idea and knowing how to find it is important. Transferring that understanding to your reading and study is also important.

1　A　Hydraulics

Hydraulics is the study of the forces and motions in liquids, such as water and oils. Pumps, propellers, and turbines are examples of hydraulic machinery. In a centrifugal pump, an impeller imparts tangential velocity to the fluid through vanes that are driven by an external power source, and the vanes increase the kinetic energy, and sometimes the pressure, of the flow. The high-speed flow leaving the impeller is then slowed through a set of diffusing passages in which the kinetic energy is converted to flow energy and the outflow pressure increases. In ship propellers, the difference in pressure between the forward and backward sides of the blades creates thrust, which propels the vessel through the water.

Waterwheels date from Roman times when water flowing past a rotating paddle wheel was used to produce power for milling; however, these waterwheels extracted only a small portion of the energy in a stream. Modern hydraulic power-producing machines, known as turbines, work on different principles. Their design depends on the height between the reservoir and the turbine outflow. For a large height difference, or head, and low flow rates, the Pelton wheel or turbine is used in which the water flowing down a pipe, or penstock, accelerates through a nozzle at the bottom. The high-speed water is then directed onto a wheel. Pelton turbines are typically used if the head is greater than about 500 feet (150 meters). For smaller heads, the Francis turbine, which is the counterpart of a centrifugal pump, is commonly used. Water flows into the turbine in a radial direction and is discharged at lower pressure nearly axially downward. For low heads and high flow rates, vertically installed propeller or Kaplan turbines are used. Whereas in ship propellers the turning propeller moves the water, propeller turbines use flowing water to turn the propeller. Another hydraulic machine, the torque converter of an automobile, permits smooth transmission of power from the engine to the drive shaft.

Fluid forces transmitted in a pipe have many applications. The hydraulic brake in a car depends on the pressure exerted on a fluid reservoir by the brake pedal. This force is then transmitted through oil lines to move the brake shoes. Power steering uses a hydraulic system to magnify the torque applied to the steering wheel to turn the car. Hydraulic power is also used in airplanes to move control surfaces, such as the tail and rudder.

Reading Time _____

Recalling Facts

1. In a centrifugal pump, the device that forces fluid to move is called
   - ❑ a. a turbine.
   - ❑ b. an impeller.
   - ❑ c. a rotating paddle.

2. Power for milling during Roman times was created by
   - ❑ a. windmills.
   - ❑ b. steam.
   - ❑ c. waterwheels.

3. Modern hydraulic power-producing machines are called
   - ❑ a. reservoirs.
   - ❑ b. turbines.
   - ❑ c. propulsion devices.

4. Ship propellers work on the principle that
   - ❑ a. flowing water turns the propeller.
   - ❑ b. the turning propeller moves the water.
   - ❑ c. water seeks its own level.

5. A hydraulic machine used in an automobile, the torque converter,
   - ❑ a. permits smooth transmission of power from the engine to the drive shaft.
   - ❑ b. allows gasoline to be converted to energy.
   - ❑ c. controls the electrical system.

Understanding Ideas

6. All hydraulic machines depend on
   - ❑ a. pulleys.
   - ❑ b. electrical energy.
   - ❑ c. the movement of fluids.

7. Modern hydraulic technology is based on
   - ❑ a. new concepts of water power.
   - ❑ b. age-old concepts of putting moving water to work.
   - ❑ c. the discovery of kinetic energy.

8. You can conclude from the article that a major difference between ancient and modern hydraulic machines is the
   - ❑ a. amount of energy extracted.
   - ❑ b. size of the machinery.
   - ❑ c. amount of work required.

9. Hydraulic machines
   - ❑ a. have widespread applications.
   - ❑ b. are used primarily in the transportation industry.
   - ❑ c. are useful only where there is a natural water supply.

10. You can conclude from the article that the higher the speed of water in hydraulic machines, the
   - ❑ a. more thrust is produced.
   - ❑ b. more energy is produced.
   - ❑ c. less energy is produced.

The Shipmill That Saved a City

In the fifth century A.D., the great Roman Empire fell to barbarians. The city of Rome itself was sacked by the Visigoths in 410 and by the Vandals in 455. By the sixth century, all that remained of Rome's imperial glory was the Eastern Roman Empire, whose capital was Byzantium in what later became Turkey.

The great Byzantine general Belisarius embarked on a campaign to reconquer Italy for the empire. In A.D. 536, Belisarius and his army were trapped in Rome by the Goths. Hoping to starve out the Byzantine army, the Goths cut the water supply to the mills that ground the city's corn.

Belisarius came up with a brilliant idea. He had the mills mounted on barges and floated in the River Tiber, which ran through the city. The Tiber was too large a river for the Goths to divert. The mills ground away, producing cornmeal for the city's inhabitants. The Goths tried to destroy Belisarius's invention by floating trees and other large debris down the river to catch in and stop or break the shipmill's paddles. The clever Belisarius, however, had a large chain installed upstream of the shipmill to catch anything thrown into the river. The city held out.

1. Recognizing Words in Context

Find the word *ground* in the passage. One definition below is a *synonym* for that word; it means the same or almost the same thing. One definition is an *antonym;* it has the opposite or nearly opposite meaning. The other has a completely different meaning. Label the definitions S for *synonym*, A for *antonym*, and D for *different*.

_____ a. earth

_____ b. restored

_____ c. pulverized

2. Distinguishing Fact from Opinion

Two of the statements below present *facts*, which can be proved correct. The other statement is an *opinion,* which expresses someone's thoughts or beliefs. Label the statements F for *fact* and O for *opinion*.

_____ a. The Goths cut off the water supply to the city's cornmills.

_____ b. Belisarius was clever.

_____ c. Belisarius had mills placed on barges and floated in the river.

3. **Keeping Events in Order**

Label the statements below 1, 2, and 3 to show the order in which the events happened.

_____ a. Belisarius and his army were trapped in Rome by the Goths.

_____ b. Belisarius invented a shipmill by having mills floated in the river on barges.

_____ c. The Goths cut off the water supply to the city's cornmills.

4. **Making Correct Inferences**

Two of the statements below are correct *inferences,* or reasonable guesses. They are based on information in the passage. The other statement is an incorrect, or faulty, inference. Label the statements C for *correct* inference and F for *faulty* inference.

_____ a. Watermills for grinding corn played an important role in the life of Rome.

_____ b. Belisarius had abilities that went beyond battle skills.

_____ c. Corn was the only food the Romans had.

5. **Understanding Main Ideas**

One of the statements below expresses the main idea of the passage. One statement is too general, or too broad. The other explains only part of the passage; it is too narrow. Label the statements M for *main idea*, B for *too broad*, and N for *too narrow*.

_____ a. Belisarius, a Byzantine general, invented a shipmill to counter his enemies' attempts to starve out his army.

_____ b. The Goths cut the water supply to Rome's cornmills.

_____ c. Watermills played a major part in the ancient economy, especially for grinding corn.

Correct Answers, Part A _____

Correct Answers, Part B _____

Total Correct Answers _____

In the second half of the twentieth century, the Reverend Billy Graham was known the world over for his entertaining style of evangelism. Beginning in 1944, this Christian evangelist conducted crusades, or preaching campaigns, in North America, the Far East, Europe, and Africa. In the 1980s, he was allowed to preach in China, the Soviet Union, and some Eastern European countries—a noteworthy achievement since, at the time, those nations did not support religious freedom for their peoples.

William Franklin Graham was born near Charlotte, North Carolina, on November 7, 1918. He had wanted to be a baseball player, but it was not to be. After being converted at a revival meeting when he was 16, he decided on a career of preaching. He studied at Bob Jones College and the Florida Bible Institute. After graduation, he was ordained a Baptist minister. Following ordination, he attended Wheaton College in Illinois. Today the college is the home of the Billy Graham Center, an institution for the study of religion. Graham served briefly as pastor of a congregation in Western Springs, Illinois.

In 1949, Reverend Graham became a vice-president of the Youth for Christ International. This evangelical organization had been formed after World War II. In the same year, he held an eight-week series of tent meetings in Los Angeles.

During the 1950s and 1960s, Reverend Graham preached a great number of campaigns all over the United States. His radio program, *Hour of Decision,* was heard by millions around the world. His first campaigns outside the United States were in England and continental Europe in 1954 and 1955.

Reverend Graham used modern communications to put forward his conservative brand of Christianity. Many of his campaigns were televised. The success of the campaigns enabled him to establish the Billy Graham Evangelistic Association in Minneapolis, Minnesota. From 1949 to 1951, he was also president of Northwestern Schools, a fundamentalist institution in Minneapolis.

In addition to the campaigns, Reverend Graham wrote a newspaper column, produced films, and published a number of books. He has been a friend and confidante of several United States presidents, beginning with Harry Truman in 1949.

Reverend Graham continued his preaching crusades in the 1980s and 1990s, using satellite technology to reach people in many countries. Unfortunately, some evangelists were involved in scandals in the late 1980s. Some of them were imprisoned for their misdeeds. Graham's reputation, however, has remained untarnished.

Reading Time _____

Recalling Facts

1. Billy Graham is famous for his
   - ❏ a. preaching crusades.
   - ❏ b. satellite technology.
   - ❏ c. organizational ability.

2. Billy Graham was ordained a
   - ❏ a. Catholic priest.
   - ❏ b. Baptist clergyman.
   - ❏ c. Protestant minister.

3. The Billy Graham Center is
   - ❏ a. a Baptist church.
   - ❏ b. a religious museum.
   - ❏ c. an institution for the study of religion.

4. In addition to being a minister, Billy Graham was
   - ❏ a. an airplane pilot.
   - ❏ b. a newspaper columnist.
   - ❏ c. an actor.

5. Billy Graham's brand of Christianity is considered
   - ❏ a. conservative.
   - ❏ b. daring.
   - ❏ c. untraditional.

Understanding Ideas

6. You can conclude from the article that an evangelist is someone who
   - ❏ a. preaches on the radio.
   - ❏ b. appears on television.
   - ❏ c. preaches the gospel.

7. Billy Graham was allowed to preach in nations that did not support religious freedom, which suggests that
   - ❏ a. he was greatly respected.
   - ❏ b. those nations were ready to convert to Christianity.
   - ❏ c. he liked to travel.

8. Billy Graham's fame outside the United States is largely due to
   - ❏ a. advances in transportation.
   - ❏ b. modern communications.
   - ❏ c. successful ad campaigns.

9. You can conclude from the article that Billy Graham is
   - ❏ a. introverted.
   - ❏ b. shy.
   - ❏ c. outgoing.

10. The term *tent meetings* refers to
    - ❏ a. business seminars.
    - ❏ b. religious gatherings.
    - ❏ c. fund-raising events.

Although Reverend Billy Graham has been an advisor to every United States president—both Democrat and Republican—since Harry Truman, he was closer to President Richard M. Nixon than to any other president. Graham delivered the opening prayer at Nixon's inauguration in 1969. He gave thanks that "in Thy sovereignty Thou hast permitted Richard Nixon to lead us at this momentous hour of our history."

In 1970, less than three weeks after members of the National Guard shot to death four students at Kent State University in Ohio, President Nixon appeared at a Billy Graham rally at the University of Tennessee. The president hoped to distance himself from the tragedy at Kent State and to regain the support of students.

When President Nixon was under fire in 1973 over the break-in at Democratic National Committee headquarters, Graham stood by the president. When transcripts of secretly taped White House conversations appeared in print, however, Graham admitted that reading the president's conversations was "a profoundly disturbing and disappointing experience." He did say, though, that he had "no intention of forsaking [the president] now." Even after Nixon was forced to resign as president in 1974, the two men remained friends. At President Nixon's funeral in 1994, Reverend Graham delivered the eulogy for his old friend.

1. **Recognizing Words in Context**

   Find the word *distance* in the passage. One definition below is a *synonym* for that word; it means the same or almost the same thing. One definition is an *antonym;* it has the opposite or nearly opposite meaning. The other has a completely different meaning. Label the definitions S for *synonym*, A for *antonym*, and D for *different*.

   _____ a. length

   _____ b. approach

   _____ c. separate

2. **Distinguishing Fact from Opinion**

   Two of the statements below present *facts,* which can be proved correct. The other statement is an *opinion,* which expresses someone's thoughts or beliefs. Label the statements F for *fact* and O for *opinion*.

   _____ a. Reverend Graham delivered the opening prayer at President Nixon's inauguration.

   _____ b. The president's conversations were disappointing and disturbing to Billy Graham.

   _____ c. Nixon appeared at a Billy Graham rally at the University of Tennessee.

3. **Keeping Events in Order**

   Label the statements below 1, 2, and 3 to show the order in which the events happened.

   _____ a. President Nixon attended a Billy Graham rally at the University of Tennessee.

   _____ b. Four students at Kent State University were killed by members of the National Guard.

   _____ c. Nixon came under attack over a break-in at Democratic National Committee headquarters.

4. **Making Correct Inferences**

   Two of the statements below are correct *inferences*, or reasonable guesses. They are based on information in the passage. The other statement is an incorrect, or faulty, inference. Label the statements C for *correct* inference and F for *faulty* inference.

   _____ a. Reverend Graham stood by President Nixon because he believed in his friend's innocence.

   _____ b. Reverend Graham is loyal to his friends.

   _____ c. A president's political party holds no importance for Reverend Graham.

5. **Understanding Main Ideas**

   One of the statements below expresses the main idea of the passage. One statement is too general, or too broad. The other explains only part of the passage; it is too narrow. Label the statements M for *main idea*, B for *too broad*, and N for *too narrow*.

   _____ a. Reverend Billy Graham was a loyal friend to President Nixon.

   _____ b. Reverend Graham has been an advisor to every president since Harry Truman.

   _____ c. Reverend Graham delivered the eulogy at President Nixon's funeral.

   Correct Answers, Part A _____

   Correct Answers, Part B _____

   Total Correct Answers _____

20

Fairs and Expositions

Although the terms are now used almost interchangeably, fairs and expositions, or exhibitions, have traditionally not been the same. A fair is a temporary market at which buyers and sellers gather to transact business. An exposition is a display of works of art, science, or industry to stimulate public interest. Expositions promote manufactured products, expand trade, or illustrate progress in a variety of areas. The factor that fairs and expositions have in common is they are both temporary, lasting from a few days to several months. A world's fair, which is really an exposition, usually lasts about six or more months. If it becomes permanent in any location, it would be an amusement, or theme, park. A permanent exhibition of paintings is considered a museum.

The primary purpose of a fair is to promote buying and selling. Fairs may have associated with them all kinds of entertainment—sideshows, musical presentations, gambling concessions, and carnival rides—but their main purpose is to function as a large market. Prior to the twentieth century, most fairs offered a great variety of products and services for sale. Since 1900, the most popular type of fair has become that devoted to a single industry as, for example, the Frankfurt Book Fair held in Germany.

Fairs originated to solve the problem of distribution of goods. As long ago as 1000 B.C., it was quite common for caravans of merchants to converge on cities in Egypt, Syria, Palestine, and Mesopotamia during religious festivals when many people would be together in a holiday mood. (The word *fair* comes from a Latin word meaning "holiday.") They brought commodities from faraway places in India, Africa, and Central Asia. By appearing on a regular, if infrequent, basis, merchants could concentrate supply and demand in a certain place at a specific time. As centuries passed, the religious aspect of the feast diminished, and the commercial aspect dominated.

With the disintegration of the Roman Empire in the fifth century A.D., most commerce ceased for about 200 years. But in the Muslim world of North Africa and the Middle East, as well as India, fairs continued to flourish. Muslims controlled much of the shipping in the Mediterranean, the Red Sea, and the Persian Gulf. Exotic goods found their way from China, India, and Southeast Asia to these fairs. The merchants also carried commodities from North Africa and the Middle East to India and China.

Reading Time _____

Recalling Facts

1. The primary purpose of a fair is to
   - ❏ a. amuse patrons.
   - ❏ b. promote buying and selling.
   - ❏ c. create a museum.

2. The word *fair* comes from a Latin word meaning
   - ❏ a. merchandise.
   - ❏ b. holiday.
   - ❏ c. entertainment.

3. Fairs originated to
   - ❏ a. provide for the distribution of goods.
   - ❏ b. give merchants an opportunity to celebrate.
   - ❏ c. promote the farming industry.

4. The most popular kind of fair today is
   - ❏ a. the amusement fair.
   - ❏ b. the religious fair.
   - ❏ c. devoted to one industry.

5. The disintegration of the Roman Empire brought about
   - ❏ a. an increase in trade.
   - ❏ b. a slight decrease in trade.
   - ❏ c. an end to almost all trade.

Understanding Ideas

6. Fairs were originally
   - ❏ a. religious in nature.
   - ❏ b. solely for entertainment.
   - ❏ c. commercial in nature.

7. It is likely that prior to the emergence of fairs, demand for foreign goods
   - ❏ a. exceeded supply.
   - ❏ b. did not exist.
   - ❏ c. lagged behind supply.

8. You can conclude from the article that commercial fairs benefited
   - ❏ a. both the buyer and the seller.
   - ❏ b. the buyer rather than the seller.
   - ❏ c. the seller rather than the buyer.

9. The article implies that prior to the fifth century, the Roman Empire
   - ❏ a. was disinterested in commerce.
   - ❏ b. controlled commerce.
   - ❏ c. outlawed foreign trade.

10. As trade among countries increased, fairs probably
   - ❏ a. became less popular.
   - ❏ b. became more popular.
   - ❏ c. ceased.

Come to the Fair

It was a beautiful summer day in Chicago. Catherine was almost skipping as she walked beside her parents through the gate of the World's Columbian Exposition. Chicago had campaigned hard for the honor of holding the event marking the 400th anniversary of Christopher Columbus's first visit to America, just barely edging out New York City.

As Catherine and her parents entered the fairgrounds, they saw a dazzling "White City" in the style of classic European architecture. The city's columns, domes, arches, staircases, and fountains were painted a gleaming white.

Inside was a world of the future. Catherine stared openmouthed in amazement at massive machines, an electric stove, product displays, and art from all 48 states and other nations as well. She saw the first fiberglass, the first zippers, and the first American picture postcards. Her parents were amazed by the newest advance in telephoning—long-distance telephone calls.

After touring the exhibits, Catherine and her parents went out to the Midway. They laughed nervously as they rode George Ferris's giant wheel, which carried them 205 feet (62 meters) above the ground. Catherine gasped at the panoramic view of the White City far below. The year 1893 was a wonderful time to be alive and in Chicago!

1. Recognizing Words in Context

Find the word *advance* in the passage. One definition below is a *synonym* for that word; it means the same or almost the same thing. One definition is an *antonym;* it has the opposite or nearly opposite meaning. The other has a completely different meaning. Label the definitions S for *synonym*, A for *antonym*, and D for *different*.

_____ a. forward step

_____ b. regression

_____ c. proceed

2. Distinguishing Fact from Opinion

Two of the statements below present *facts*, which can be proved correct. The other statement is an *opinion*, which expresses someone's thoughts or beliefs. Label the statements F for *fact* and O for *opinion*.

_____ a. The World's Columbian Exposition of 1893 displayed the first fiberglass.

_____ b. The World's Columbian Exposition of 1893 was the most elaborate ever held.

_____ c. George Ferris designed the Ferris wheel for the World's Columbian Exposition of 1893.

3. Keeping Events in Order

Two of the statements below describe events that happened at the same time. The other statement describes an event that happened before or after those events. Label them S for *same time*, B for *before*, and A for *after*.

_____ a. Catherine and her parents laughed nervously.

_____ b. Catherine and her parents went out onto the Midway.

_____ c. The giant wheel carried them 205 feet (62 meters) above the ground.

4. Making Correct Inferences

Two of the statements below are correct *inferences*, or reasonable guesses. They are based on information in the passage. The other statement is an incorrect, or faulty, inference. Label the statements C for *correct* inference and F for *faulty* inference.

_____ a. The World's Columbian Exposition of 1893 was notable for its vision of America's future.

_____ b. Many things that are commonplace today were first introduced at the 1893 Exposition.

_____ c. The 1893 Exposition primarily offered entertainment over education.

5. Understanding Main Ideas

One of the statements below expresses the main idea of the passage. One statement is too general, or too broad. The other explains only part of the passage; it is too narrow. Label the statements M for *main idea*, B for *too broad*, and N for *too narrow*.

_____ a. Expositions show people the future.

_____ b. Fairgoers to the World's Columbian Exposition of 1893 saw many new products and a world of the future in a brief time.

_____ c. Fairgoers saw a vast "White City" in the style of classic European architecture.

Correct Answers, Part A _____

Correct Answers, Part B _____

Total Correct Answers _____

4   A   Wildlife Conservation

The preservation of wildlife greatly depends upon water and soil conservation. All native plants and animals constitute the wildlife of a region and are a product of the land resources and habitat conditions. Wild animals must have food, water, and shelter. Destroying the forests, marshes, ponds, and grasslands destroys their food and water supplies and the places in which they live.

Of the original native wildlife of the United States, many species are now extinct. These include the passenger pigeon, the Carolina parakeet, the great auk, the Labrador duck, the Pallas cormorant, the dusky seaside sparrow, and the heath hen. Mammals gone forever include the Eastern elk, the Plains wolf, the sea mink, and the Bad Lands bighorn. Many smaller birds and mammals have also become extinct in the wild. Populations of the ivory-billed woodpecker and the California condor no longer exist in the wild in the United States.

The number of moose, caribou, wild sheep and goats, and grizzly and Alaska brown bears grows smaller every year. Much wildlife is now protected by law from overhunting and overfishing. However, if the destruction of their natural homes continues, many species will be unable to survive.

The United States Fish and Wildlife Service maintains a list of endangered and threatened species of the United States. Environmental concerns for a variety of reptiles, amphibians, small fishes, insects, and mollusks are reflected in the number of species classed as threatened or endangered.

The Endangered Species Act has been effective for preserving some species. For example, the American alligator had been reduced to a relatively small number by the early 1960s due to illegal hunting for hides and meat. After 20 years of protection, the species recovered to such a large extent in many parts of its range that it led to a relaxation of the laws in the 1980s so that limited hunting was permitted.

Worldwide, the International Union for Conservation of Nature and Natural Resources keeps track of species threatened with extinction. Endangered species include many of the world's great cats, whales, certain species of rhinoceros, tapirs, and many other mammals, birds, and reptiles. Housing and other facilities needed by an expanding human population are encroaching on their habitats.

Many species are the victims of the illegal pet trade and of the trade in exotic pelts and skins. The increasing availability of guns and poisons is responsible for the extermination of other species.

Reading Time _____

Recalling Facts

1. Wildlife preservation depends on
   - ❏ a. reservations.
   - ❏ b. conservation.
   - ❏ c. interpretation.

2. Animals that have become extinct
   - ❏ a. no longer exist.
   - ❏ b. are in danger of disappearing.
   - ❏ c. still exist in zoos.

3. Extinct birds include
   - ❏ a. sea minks.
   - ❏ b. passenger pigeons.
   - ❏ c. parrots.

4. The agency responsible for wildlife conservation in the United States is the
   - ❏ a. Association for the Prevention of Cruelty to Animals.
   - ❏ b. National Forestry Service.
   - ❏ c. United States Fish and Wildlife Service.

5. A once-protected species that has grown greatly in number is the
   - ❏ a. American alligator.
   - ❏ b. Plains wolf.
   - ❏ c. Carolina parakeet.

Understanding Ideas

6. You can conclude from the article that the present danger to wildlife
   - ❏ a. is mainly from overhunting and overfishing.
   - ❏ b. is from destruction of their habitats.
   - ❏ c. will lessen as time goes by.

7. It is too late to save creatures that are
   - ❏ a. threatened.
   - ❏ b. endangered.
   - ❏ c. extinct.

8. The biggest problem facing wildlife conservationists is
   - ❏ a. how to keep track of endangered species.
   - ❏ b. saving wildlife while meeting the needs of an expanding human population.
   - ❏ c. whether to save endangered mammals or birds.

9. Wildlife conservation is a problem
   - ❏ a. mainly in the United States.
   - ❏ b. mainly in Africa and Asia.
   - ❏ c. all around the world.

10. You can conclude from the article that hunting wild animals
   - ❏ a. helps control the size of animal populations.
   - ❏ b. is never allowed in the United States.
   - ❏ c. is no longer a popular sport.

Saving the Red Wolf

Red wolves once roamed freely throughout the southern United States. Then came settlers who cleared the land for homes and farms, greatly reducing the wolves' habitat. Fearing the wolves, the settlers shot, poisoned, and trapped them vigorously, decimating the wolf population. Between 1932 and 1964, with the wolf classified as a harmful predator, state and federal animal control agents destroyed thousands more. Under pressure, the wolves began to breed with coyotes, a close relative.

By the 1970s, conservationists at the U.S. Fish and Wildlife Service realized that red wolves were close to extinction. They captured about four hundred wild wolf-type animals and tested them. Only forty were pure red wolves. These animals were sent to a zoo for a breeding program, and soon their numbers began to increase.

By 1986, seven young wolves were ready for release. Conservationists chose a wildlife refuge in North Carolina with thick underbrush for cover and plenty of the wolves' favorite foods—rabbits, squirrels, insects, and fish. Two of the wolves died within a short time, but the rest survived. Two years later, they were joined by eight more wolves raised in captivity. Thus, the red wolf became one of the first animals to be saved from extinction and returned to the wild.

1. **Recognizing Words in Context**

    Find the word *decimating* in the passage. One definition below is a *synonym* for that word; it means the same or almost the same thing. One definition is an *antonym*; it has the opposite or nearly opposite meaning. The other has a completely different meaning. Label the definitions S for *synonym*, A for *antonym*, and D for *different*.

    _____ a. saving

    _____ b. reducing

    _____ c. discouraging

2. **Distinguishing Fact from Opinion**

    Two of the statements below present *facts*, which can be proved correct. The other statement is an *opinion*, which expresses someone's thoughts or beliefs. Label the statements F for *fact* and O for *opinion*.

    _____ a. Settlers shot, poisoned, and trapped wolves.

    _____ b. Between 1932 and 1964, the wolf was classified as a harmful predator.

    _____ c. People feared wolves.

3. **Keeping Events in Order**

   Label the statements below 1, 2, and 3 to show the order in which the events happened.

   _____ a. Animal control agents killed thousands of wolves.

   _____ b. Conservationists trapped and tested four hundred wolf-type animals.

   _____ c. Wolves bred in captivity were released in North Carolina.

4. **Making Correct Inferences**

   Two of the statements below are correct *inferences*, or reasonable guesses. They are based on information in the passage. The other statement is an incorrect, or faulty, inference. Label the statements C for *correct* inference and F for *faulty* inference.

   _____ a. Government policies against wolves almost destroyed the breed.

   _____ b. Red wolves are dangerous to people and livestock.

   _____ c. Attitudes toward wolves have changed in the last 35 years.

5. **Understanding Main Ideas**

   One of the statements below expresses the main idea of the passage. One statement is too general, or too broad. The other explains only part of the passage; it is too narrow. Label the statements M for *main idea*, B for *too broad*, and N for *too narrow*.

   _____ a. Red wolves almost became extinct.

   _____ b. By the 1970s, conservationists at the U.S. Fish and Wildlife Service realized that red wolves were close to extinction.

   _____ c. After years of destruction, the red wolf was saved from extinction by conservationists and returned to the wild.

Correct Answers, Part A _____

Correct Answers, Part B _____

Total Correct Answers _____

Modern industry depends on abrasives, the hard, sharp, and rough substances used to rub and wear away softer, less resistant surfaces. Without them, it would be impossible to make machine parts that fit precisely together, and there would be no automobiles, airplanes, spacecraft, home appliances, or machine tools. Abrasives include the grit in household cleansing powder, coated forms such as emery boards and sandpaper, honing stones for knife sharpening, and grinding wheels. Numerous substances such as silicon carbide and diamonds used in industry to shape and polish are also abrasives.

Hardness and toughness are important characteristics in determining the usefulness of an abrasive. For example, an abrasive must be harder than the material it grinds. Toughness determines an abrasive's useful life. The ideal abrasive grain resharpens itself in use by breakdown of its dulled cutting edge to expose yet another cutting edge within.

Because it is the hardest of all substances, diamond is a particularly good natural abrasive. Diamonds that are unsuitable for jewelry are crushed into various sizes for use in grinding wheels, polishing powders, abrasive belts, and polishing disks. Corundum, a naturally occurring form of aluminum oxide, is used primarily to polish and grind glass. Emery, another form of aluminum oxide, is found in nature as small crystals embedded in iron oxide. It is most often used in emerycloth sandpaper and emery boards for filing fingernails. Garnet, noted for its toughness, is widely used, particularly for coated abrasive products in the woodworking, leather, and shoe industries. Flint, or flint quartz, is the abrasive most commonly used to make sandpaper. It is mined, crushed, and bonded to paper or cloth. Quartz, the major ingredient of sandstone, is largely responsible for the abrasive qualities of sandstone. Quartz, by itself in the form of sand, is used for sandblasting. Pumice, the cooled and hardened frothy part of volcanic lava, is a familiar mild abrasive used in polishing metals and finishing furniture, and in scouring powders and soaps.

Manufactured abrasives include glass beads and metal shot. Both are often blasted at machines and other objects to clean them. Steel wool, which is made by combing steel wire, is a common and widely used cleaning and surface-finishing material.

Almost all abrasives are crushed to a specific particle size before being used to make a product. The crushing method, because it affects crystal strength, also helps determine the possible uses for the resulting abrasive.

Reading Time _____

Recalling Facts

1. The usefulness of an abrasive is determined by its
   - ❏ a. naturalness.
   - ❏ b. ability to break down.
   - ❏ c. hardness and toughness.

2. The hardest of all substances is
   - ❏ a. diamond.
   - ❏ b. emery.
   - ❏ c. flint.

3. Sandpaper is made from
   - ❏ a. steel.
   - ❏ b. flint.
   - ❏ c. pumice.

4. The ideal abrasive
   - ❏ a. is inexpensive.
   - ❏ b. is crushed to make a product.
   - ❏ c. resharpens itself in use.

5. An abrasive must be
   - ❏ a. harder than the material it grinds.
   - ❏ b. softer than the material it grinds.
   - ❏ c. easy to manufacture.

Understanding Ideas

6. You can conclude from the article that the abrasive used in emery boards is
   - ❏ a. harder than fingernails.
   - ❏ b. softer than fingernails.
   - ❏ c. harder than industrial abrasives.

7. Not all diamonds are used for abrasives because some are
   - ❏ a. too hard to crush.
   - ❏ b. not hard enough.
   - ❏ c. more valuable as gems.

8. The article wants you to understand that abrasives
   - ❏ a. can be dangerous.
   - ❏ b. have a wide variety of uses.
   - ❏ c. are of limited usefulness.

9. You can conclude from the article that too hard an abrasive
   - ❏ a. may cause scratching.
   - ❏ b. will wear away too quickly.
   - ❏ c. will have no effect.

10. The article suggests that people's lives without abrasives would be
    - ❏ a. much improved.
    - ❏ b. quite limited.
    - ❏ c. no different.

5 B   Barton's Magic Abrasive

In 1878 in Philadelphia, a sandpaper maker named Henry Hudson Barton sent samples of sandpaper to the local woodworkers and carriage makers. Within hours they were clamoring for more; the new sandpaper was finer, harder, and longer-lasting than any they had ever tried. What was this stuff? Barton would not tell. He called it Barton's Magic Abrasive.

Barton's secret was garnet but not just any garnet. Formerly a jeweler, he knew gems as well as he knew sandpaper. When a friend showed him a sample of garnet from Gore Mountain in New York's Adirondack Mountains, Barton quickly grasped the implications for his business. He purchased all the garnet he could. When demand grew, he visited the site and saw huge pockets of garnet, some as big as two feet (0.6 meters) across, embedded in rock. The garnet was gem quality but so hard it fractured easily. Few pieces were large enough for jewelry; the garnet was perfect for abrasives.

Barton purchased the mountain. He began a mining operation and was soon producing some of the world's finest garnet paper. Today Barton's mining operations produce not only garnet paper and cloth but also abrasives for grinding TV tubes, grains for sandblasting, and garnet for many other industrial applications.

1. Recognizing Words in Context

Find the word *implications* in the passage. One definition below is a *synonym* for that word; it means the same or almost the same thing. One definition is an *antonym;* it has the opposite or nearly opposite meaning. The other has a completely different meaning. Label the definitions S for *synonym,* A for *antonym,* and D for *different.*

_____ a. possible significance

_____ b. insignificance

_____ c. expense

2. Distinguishing Fact from Opinion

Two of the statements below present *facts,* which can be proved correct. The other statement is an *opinion,* which expresses someone's thoughts or beliefs. Label the statements F for *fact* and O for *opinion.*

_____ a. Gore Mountain contained garnet deposits.

_____ b. Barton's sandpaper was better than any other.

_____ c. Some pockets of garnet were two feet (0.6 meters) across.

3. Keeping Events in Order

Label the statements below 1, 2, and 3 to show the order in which the events happened.

_____ a. Henry Barton purchased Gore Mountain.

_____ b. Henry Barton made Barton's Magic Abrasive.

_____ c. Barton began his own mining operation.

4. Making Correct Inferences

Two of the statements below are correct *inferences*, or reasonable guesses. They are based on information in the passage. The other statement is an incorrect, or faulty, inference. Label the statements C for *correct* inference and F for *faulty* inference.

_____ a. Demand for garnet products remains high today.

_____ b. Garnet is an excellent industrial abrasive.

_____ c. Today, garnet is not as important to industry as it was in Barton's day.

5. Understanding Main Ideas

One of the statements below expresses the main idea of the passage. One statement is too general, or too broad. The other explains only part of the passage; it is too narrow. Label the statements M for *main idea,* B for *too broad,* and N for *too narrow.*

_____ a. Henry Barton pioneered the use of garnet as an industrial abrasive.

_____ b. The Gore Mountain site contained huge pockets of garnet.

_____ c. Garnets make good abrasives.

Correct Answers, Part A _____

Correct Answers, Part B _____

Total Correct Answers _____

Investigating the Brain

Over the years, scientists have tried to unravel the brain's vast complexity and to develop simple, meaningful theories about how it works. Some experimental data supports the view that the brain is divided into specialized areas—areas that control vision, touch, movement, memory, and so on. On the other hand, there is also evidence to indicate that the brain at all times functions as a whole and that one region can perform several tasks and so can compensate for the loss of or damage to another region.

Scientists can study the brain by analyzing its electrical activity, or brain waves, using a device called an electroencephalograph (EEG). The EEG report displays line graphs made up of characteristic wave patterns. These wave patterns can reveal a person's state of mind and the brain's state of health; they can also help scientists study how the brain works. The device's effectiveness as a research tool is limited, however, because it records only a small sample of electrical activity from the surface of the brain. Many of the more complex functions of the brain, such as those that underlie emotions and thought, cannot be related closely to EEG patterns.

Some current research is aimed at understanding the brain on the micro-molecular level. Such research includes the study of so-called second messenger systems, involving long-lasting chemicals that modulate responses within the brain; the cloning of neurotransmitter receptors; the study of the regrowth of nerve fibers; and the identification of possible growth-promoting substances.

Another field of research involves the brain's role in a human's primitive inborn sense of direction. Researchers have found tiny magnetic particles in the human brain that they speculate may help a person navigate using the Earth's magnetic fields. Such particles had previously been found in other animals, such as pigeons and honeybees.

Other research is aimed at deepening the understanding of normal and diseased brain states. These studies are based on applications of scans that can provide color-coded maps showing which parts of the brain are used during the performance of different tasks. Related research efforts are aimed at discovering the biochemical basis of mental illness.

Some neuroscientists are collaborating with linguists and psychologists in order to understand how computers and brains are similar and how they are different. Although the brain does have some elements in common with a computer, the brain can accomplish far more than can any computer.

Reading Time _____

Recalling Facts

1. An electroencephalograph (EEG) measures brain
   - ❏ a. responses.
   - ❏ b. waves.
   - ❏ c. transmissions.

2. EEG patterns tell scientists about
   - ❏ a. complex brain functions.
   - ❏ b. simple brain functions.
   - ❏ c. brain growth.

3. Tiny magnetic particles have been found in the brain that may help a person
   - ❏ a. navigate.
   - ❏ b. talk.
   - ❏ c. play a musical instrument.

4. Parts of the brain used during different tasks
   - ❏ a. appear on EEG report displays.
   - ❏ b. can be color-coded on maps.
   - ❏ c. have yet to be studied.

5. The human brain and a computer
   - ❏ a. have nothing in common.
   - ❏ b. function in the same way.
   - ❏ c. share some similarities.

Understanding Ideas

6. The article wants you to understand that scientists
   - ❏ a. are bored with brain research.
   - ❏ b. disagree about how the brain works.
   - ❏ c. are convinced that the brain functions as a whole.

7. You can conclude from the article that EEG patterns
   - ❏ a. are very basic research tools.
   - ❏ b. can be compared to sound waves.
   - ❏ c. control brain function.

8. The article suggests that an inborn sense of direction
   - ❏ a. is found only in animals.
   - ❏ b. can be found in both humans and animals.
   - ❏ c. is found only in pigeons and honeybees.

9. The article wants you to understand that computers
   - ❏ a. are more sophisticated than the human brain.
   - ❏ b. will soon outdistance the brain in accomplishments.
   - ❏ c. are inferior to the human brain.

10. The article suggests that brain research is
    - ❏ a. too diversified.
    - ❏ b. still challenging scientists.
    - ❏ c. limited to studying EEG patterns and color-coded maps.

Why do we sleep? After we've been awake for a while, a small cluster of cells at the back of the brain releases hormones that induce sleep. When these chemicals build up in the brain, neither bright lights nor noise nor will power can keep us awake. We typically fall first into a light "slow-wave" sleep, a time when an electroencephalograph will show a slow pattern with little electrical activity.

Next comes a kind of sleep known as REM, for R(apid) E(ye) M(ovement). During REM sleep, brain activity increases to a high level. Our eyes dart back and forth beneath our closed eyelids. This is a period of intense and vivid dreaming. But for the fact that chemicals released by the brain cause our bodies to be temporarily paralyzed, we would bounce around and fall out of bed. Alternating with slow-wave sleep, periods of REM sleep occur about every ninety minutes all night long.

After REM sleep comes the deepest, most restful kind of sleep: NREM, for N(on)REM. It consists of four stages in which our breathing and heart rate slow and our blood pressure and temperature fall. We sleep deeply until the next period of REM sleep. In the morning, our refreshed brains are ready to start a new day.

1. Recognizing Words in Context

Find the word *induce* in the passage. One definition below is a *synonym* for that word; it means the same or almost the same thing. One definition is an *antonym;* it has the opposite or nearly opposite meaning. The other has a completely different meaning. Label the definitions S for *synonym,* A for *antonym,* and D for *different.*

_____ a. discourage

_____ b. generate

_____ c. decrease

2. Distinguishing Fact from Opinion

Two of the statements below present *facts,* which can be proved correct. The other statement is an *opinion,* which expresses someone's thoughts or beliefs. Label the statements F for *fact* and O for *opinion.*

_____ a. Brain activity increases during REM sleep.

_____ b. Periods of REM sleep alternate with NREM sleep.

_____ c. We awake with our brains refreshed.

3. **Keeping Events in Order**

   Label the statements below 1, 2, and 3 to show the order in which the events happened.

   _____ a. We dream and our eyes dart about.

   _____ b. Deep NREM sleep occurs.

   _____ c. Sleep chemicals build up in the brain.

4. **Making Correct Inferences**

   Two of the statements below are correct *inferences,* or reasonable guesses. They are based on information in the passage. The other statement is an incorrect, or faulty, inference. Label the statements C for *correct* inference and F for *faulty* inference.

   _____ a. The release of sleep hormones is an important brain-cell activity.

   _____ b. REM sleep serves no useful purpose.

   _____ c. Sleep follows regular patterns.

5. **Understanding Main Ideas**

   One of the statements below expresses the main idea of the passage. One statement is too general, or too broad. The other explains only part of the passage; it is too narrow. Label the statements M for *main idea,* B for *too broad,* and N for *too narrow.*

   _____ a. Brain research includes research into sleep.

   _____ b. The deepest, most restful sleep is NREM sleep.

   _____ c. Researchers are gaining new insights into what happens when we sleep.

Correct Answers, Part A _____

Correct Answers, Part B _____

Total Correct Answers _____

The Age of Machines

Almost any moving mechanical device can be called a machine. Although this definition includes a variety of devices, the term *machine* generally does not pertain to devices whose primary purpose is to transmit information, such as radios, televisions, and computers. A machine may be as simple as a screw, or it may be as large and complex as an automobile. The refrigerator in a home is a machine; so are the sewing machine, the automatic garage opener, and the sump pump. The many other machines include engines, pumps, compressors, turbines, cranes, hoists, mechanical watches and clocks, and printing presses.

Some machines, called machine tools, make parts by machining them, usually by shaping material into special forms. Many are automated, and in some cases, their operation sequences are monitored by a computer. Machine tools include lathes, planers, shapers, milling machines, drill presses, and boring machines.

Robots are among the most sophisticated of all the machines. In a mass production assembly line, robots perform tasks requiring both accuracy and care; they are able to pick up a part, position it, perform a desired operation, and then send the part along the line for further processing.

The earliest complex machines date back more than 1,000 years. They include water-driven grain mills, forges, and sawmills. The age of the machine, however, began with the Industrial Revolution. During this period, steam engines replaced human and animal power with machine power. They drove machines in factories and, in locomotives and ships, improved transportation.

The invention of the internal-combustion engine in the late 1800s opened the way for modern transportation, and the development of electric motors and generators brought a new source of power to homes and industries. In most factories, however, the power came from one large electric motor and was distributed to individual machines by a series of belts and pulley systems. Engines and electric motors remained large and cumbersome until the 1920s, when the small, fractional horsepower motor was developed. Such motors enabled individual electric machines in homes and in factories to have their own motors. Computers have eased the operation and control of machines and have also advanced factory automation, often by using robots.

The development of machinery, along with advances in mass production and automation, has helped achieve the higher standard of living enjoyed by industrialized societies. Machines have significantly reduced the need for a large labor force in many industries.

Reading Time _____

Recalling Facts

1. A machine is
   - ❏ a. almost any moving mechanical device.
   - ❏ b. a device that transmits information.
   - ❏ c. any automatic device.

2. Among the most sophisticated of all machines are
   - ❏ a. refrigerators.
   - ❏ b. cash registers.
   - ❏ c. robots.

3. The machine age began with
   - ❏ a. the invention of the automobile.
   - ❏ b. the Industrial Revolution.
   - ❏ c. advances in computers.

4. Early machine power came from
   - ❏ a. steam engines.
   - ❏ b. electric motors.
   - ❏ c. gasoline generators.

5. Modern transportation was made possible by the invention of
   - ❏ a. rubber.
   - ❏ b. the internal-combustion engine.
   - ❏ c. gasoline.

Understanding Ideas

6. You can conclude from the article that complex machines
   - ❏ a. are a modern invention.
   - ❏ b. have existed for centuries.
   - ❏ c. first appeared in the 1800s.

7. The article suggests that machines have
   - ❏ a. increased the responsibilities of human workers.
   - ❏ b. created more jobs for human workers.
   - ❏ c. replaced human workers.

8. It is likely that robots perform tasks
   - ❏ a. more accurately than humans.
   - ❏ b. less accurately than humans.
   - ❏ c. about the same as humans.

9. Without machines, the standard of living would most likely be
   - ❏ a. higher in industrialized countries.
   - ❏ b. lower in industrialized countries.
   - ❏ c. no different in industrialized countries.

10. The purpose of an assembly line is to
   - ❏ a. assemble parts into a completed product.
   - ❏ b. test the usefulness of robots.
   - ❏ c. build complex machinery.

Dante Descends into the Pit

A helicopter lowered the robot explorer Dante II onto the ice a safe distance from the crater lip of Mt. Spurr, an Alaskan volcano. Dante I, which preceded Dante II, had failed only 30 feet (9 meters) into a volcano and been destroyed. Would Dante II suffer the same fate? At the scientists' signal, Dante II stretched its eight spidery legs and began a slow, careful descent into the volcano's crater. By the end of the second day, Dante had crept 350 feet (107 meters) downward.

Huge rocks broke off the volcano's walls and crashed near Dante, but the robot kept sending back information. On the fourth day, a rock damaged one of its legs, but Dante made it to the bottom of the pit. There, it analyzed the gases escaping from a vent in the crater's crust.

Dante still had to climb back out. Four hundred feet (122 meters) from the top, it hit some rubble and toppled over. A helicopter managed to attach a line to the robot and lift it partway out, but the line broke and Dante fell. Finally, a rescue team succeeded in attaching a harness to the robot, and a helicopter rescued it.

Dante could not be repaired, but project scientists were happy with the results. Work began immediately on the next generation of explorer robots.

1. Recognizing Words in Context

Find the word *kept* in the passage. One definition below is a *synonym* for that word; it means the same or almost the same thing. One definition is an *antonym*; it has the opposite or nearly opposite meaning. The other has a completely different meaning. Label the definitions S for *synonym*, A for *antonym*, and D for *different*.

_____ a. retained

_____ b. continued

_____ c. stopped

2. Distinguishing Fact from Opinion

Two of the statements below present *facts*, which can be proved correct. The other statement is an *opinion*, which expresses someone's thoughts or beliefs. Label the statements F for *fact* and O for *opinion*.

_____ a. No human could do what Dante accomplished.

_____ b. The robot traveled 350 feet (107 meters) in the first two days.

_____ c. A rock damaged one of Dante II's legs.

3. Keeping Events in Order

Label the statements below 1, 2, and 3 to show the order in which the events happened.

_____ a. The robot analyzed gases in the volcano's pit.

_____ b. Dante II hit some rubble and toppled over.

_____ c. Rocks crashed all around the robot.

4. Making Correct Inferences

Two of the statements below are correct *inferences*, or reasonable guesses. They are based on information in the passage. The other statement is an incorrect, or faulty, inference. Label the statements C for *correct* inference and F for *faulty* inference.

_____ a. Robots can work successfully in situations that are too dangerous for humans.

_____ b. Robots work independently of humans.

_____ c. Robots have important scientific uses.

5. Understanding Main Ideas

One of the statements below expresses the main idea of the passage. One statement is too general, or too broad. The other explains only part of the passage; it is too narrow. Label the statements M for *main idea*, B for *too broad*, and N for *too narrow*.

_____ a. Huge rocks crashed all around the robot, but Dante still made it to the bottom of the crater.

_____ b. The robot Dante II, which scientists used to study conditions in an active volcano, performed well although it was damaged beyond repair.

_____ c. Robots are among the most sophisticated of all machines.

Correct Answers, Part A _____

Correct Answers, Part B _____

Total Correct Answers _____

Deep Sea Communities

How some organisms cope with the harsh conditions of the ocean depths was revealed in 1977 when scientists discovered ocean-floor communities at the Galapagos Rift, at a depth of 8,200 feet (2,500 meters). The area is a major rift, or fissure, between two of the plates making up the Earth's crust. The gradual separation of the plates and the exposure of the underlying volcanic activity result in a mixing of cold seawater with hot minerals on the ocean bottom. These environmental conditions have created habitats that support deep-sea communities that were formerly unknown.

When magma, molten rock in the Earth's crust, breaks through the surface of the ocean floor, lava slowly enters the zone and cools rapidly because of the high pressure and low temperatures. Seawater circulates downward into fissures and exits the fissures laden with dissolved minerals. These hot-water vents, called smokers, contain high concentrations of iron, manganese, zinc, copper, nickel, and other metals as well as sulfur, which is also present in the form of hydrogen sulfide. Bacteria thrive on the hydrogen sulfide and form the bottom of the food chain.

The life forms huddled around these vents are characterized by large body size and high numbers of individuals, presumably because of the abundance of nutrients and the warmer temperatures. Among the remarkable finds were colonies of large red worms encased upright in white tubes anchored to the ocean floor. These worms measure up to 5 feet (1.5 meters) in length. Previously unknown species of clams, mussels, crabs, jellyfish, and other animals have been discovered in the rift communities. Newly discovered clams with white shells are among the largest clams known, some reaching lengths of more than 10 inches (25 centimeters).

Deep-sea fishes, also common around the thermal vents, live in the warm-water areas amid the clams and tube worms. A species of blind crab is a common scavenger in some areas. Although the members of rift communities have close relatives that inhabit the warmer, sunlit seas, many are species new to science.

Rift communities have been discovered on other parts of the ocean floor and presumably could occur wherever fissures are formed by the separation of the Earth's crustal plates. Some species are common to rift communities separated by thousands of miles. Each community discovered so far, however, has a unique assemblage and diversity of species. The discovery of rift communities created much excitement in deep-sea biology.

Reading Time _____

Recalling Facts

1. Molten rock in the Earth's crust is called
   - ❏ a. lava.
   - ❏ b. magma.
   - ❏ c. fissure.

2. Hot-water vents in the Earth's crust are called
   - ❏ a. smokers.
   - ❏ b. thermals.
   - ❏ c. rifts.

3. Fissures are created when
   - ❏ a. plates in the Earth's crust separate.
   - ❏ b. rifts in the Earth's plates connect.
   - ❏ c. magma breaks through the surface of the ocean floor.

4. Deep-sea communities have formed
   - ❏ a. on the Earth's crust.
   - ❏ b. around thermal vents.
   - ❏ c. in molten rock.

5. Deep-sea communities contain colonies of
   - ❏ a. fishes commonly found in rivers and streams.
   - ❏ b. previously unknown species of whales.
   - ❏ c. previously unknown species of clams, mussels, and other animals.

Understanding Ideas

6. Deep-sea life forms would probably not do well in a habitat that is
   - ❏ a. cold.
   - ❏ b. warm.
   - ❏ c. dark.

7. Minerals located around thermal vents are most likely heated by
   - ❏ a. the sun's rays.
   - ❏ b. warm sea currents.
   - ❏ c. hot lava.

8. To survive, rift communities depend on
   - ❏ a. high pressure and low temperatures.
   - ❏ b. nutrients and warmer temperatures.
   - ❏ c. coexisting with a variety of species.

9. You can conclude from the article that the life forms in rift communities
   - ❏ a. did not exist before 1977.
   - ❏ b. will eventually become extinct.
   - ❏ c. have existed for centuries.

10. Scientists were excited by the discovery of rift communities because
    - ❏ a. they proved that the sea can support a variety of life forms.
    - ❏ b. they contained life forms new to science.
    - ❏ c. of the chance to learn about volcanic activity.

Exploring the Undersea World

Until the mid-nineteenth century, scientists believed there was no life at the bottom of the sea. But in 1872, the British ship *Challenger* set out to study the world's oceans. The *Challenger* came back with specimens from the ocean floor that made people rethink their beliefs about undersea life. German, Russian, and American expeditions followed.

Early scientific explorations learned about undersea life by trawling—dropping nets to the ocean floor to see what they could scoop up. Divers were limited to shallow depths. No one had actually seen the undersea world. Then in 1934, an intrepid biologist named William Beebe made a 3,028-foot (923-meter) descent to the ocean floor off Bermuda in a bathysphere, a round, watertight chamber raised and lowered on a cable. Later, the inventor Austin Piccard developed the bathyscaphe, an undersea vehicle that could be raised and lowered by its occupants. In 1960, Piccard's grandson Jacques made a descent of 37,000 feet (11,278 meters) in an improved bathyscaphe.

Today, both manned and remote submersibles routinely descend to the bottom of the ocean for research purposes. The new submersibles have lights to illuminate the dark sea world and portholes through which scientists experience the thrill of discovering new undersea life forms.

1. Recognizing Words in Context

Find the word *intrepid* in the passage. One definition below is a *synonym* for that word; it means the same or almost the same thing. One definition is an *antonym*; it has the opposite or nearly opposite meaning. The other has a completely different meaning. Label the definitions S for *synonym*, A for *antonym*, and D for *different*.

_____ a. frightened

_____ b. fearless

_____ c. foolish

2. Distinguishing Fact from Opinion

Two of the statements below present *facts*, which can be proved correct. The other statement is an *opinion*, which expresses someone's thoughts or beliefs. Label the statements F for *fact* and O for *opinion*.

_____ a. The British ship *Challenger* was the first to study the world's oceans.

_____ b. Austin Piccard invented the bathyscaphe.

_____ c. Seeing undersea life forms is thrilling for scientists.

3. **Keeping Events in Order**

Label the statements below 1, 2, and 3 to show the order in which the events happened.

_____ a. The *Challenger* explored the world's oceans.

_____ b. William Beebe descended to the ocean floor in a bathysphere.

_____ c. Jacques Piccard descended to 37,000 feet (11,278 meters) in a bathyscaphe.

4. **Making Correct Inferences**

Two of the statements below are correct *inferences*, or reasonable guesses. They are based on information in the passage. The other statement is an incorrect, or faulty, inference. Label the statements C for *correct* inference and F for *faulty* inference.

_____ a. The ocean floor is one of the last places on Earth to be explored.

_____ b. There is little to see at the bottom of the ocean.

_____ c. Ocean exploration is an exciting field.

5. **Understanding Main Ideas**

One of the statements below expresses the main idea of the passage. One statement is too general, or too broad. The other explains only part of the passage; it is too narrow. Label the statements M for *main idea*, B for *too broad*, and N for *too narrow*.

_____ a. There is life on the ocean floor.

_____ b. The *Challenger* came back with specimens from the ocean floor that made people rethink their beliefs about undersea life.

_____ c. Beginning with the *Challenger* exploration, scientists have made steady progress in discovering undersea life.

Correct Answers, Part A _____

Correct Answers, Part B _____

Total Correct Answers _____

The Nature of Fatigue

When a person finds it difficult to go on with an activity because of a feeling of tiredness or exhaustion, that person is said to be suffering from fatigue. If the fatigue is severe enough, the person may collapse. In engineering, a metal part that gives way under repeated stress is also said to have collapsed from fatigue. Similar terms are used for living forms and for non-living forms because both can fail to perform after continuous stress and both have an endurance limit. But living forms recover from fatigue after sufficient rest, being capable of self-renewal and self-repair. Inanimate materials are irreversibly damaged by fatigue, and the objects they support such as automobiles, airplanes, and bridges can be suddenly demolished.

Persons who tend to tire easily while doing only the ordinary tasks of daily living are said to be suffering from chronic fatigue. Any of a wide variety of disorders may be responsible, but most suspect are those that deprive the body of nourishment or oxygen or that interfere with the breakdown of sugar or the elimination of waste products. Among these disorders are malnutrition and parasitic worms, heart and circulatory ailments, anemia, lung infections, kidney disorders, diabetes, and mononucleosis. Physicians also look for overuse of sedative or stimulant drugs. Although stimulants such as caffeine mask fatigue in the short run, abnormal tiredness can occur when the effect wears off, causing a craving for more of the stimulant and a general breakdown of fitness.

Another common cause of chronic fatigue is obesity. Not only is the body forced to supply and carry a larger nonworking load, it may not be getting enough oxygen for the task because fat deposits around the rib cage cause shallow breathing. In children and adolescents, chronic fatigue may signal the need for extra nourishment and rest during periods of rapid growth.

Stress may act to cause physical fatigue by keeping muscles tensed. Monotony, boredom, and too much rest also cause fatigue, and no one knows why. The fatigue of mental effort is also a mystery.

Common causes of tiredness at work are poorly fitting equipment, inadequate ventilation, boredom, emotional stress, and visual strain. Many workers complain of visual fatigue from using computers all day. Burnout, a disabling exhaustion similar to battle fatigue, is associated with prolonged working hours under stressful conditions, a feeling of inadequacy or insecurity, and strong emotions of rage, helplessness, and despair.

Reading Time _____

Recalling Facts

1. Fatigue occurs
   - ❏ a. solely in inanimate materials.
   - ❏ b. solely in living forms.
   - ❏ c. in both living and nonliving forms.

2. Fatigue irreversibly damages
   - ❏ a. living forms.
   - ❏ b. inanimate materials.
   - ❏ c. living and nonliving forms.

3. Tiredness that lasts over a long period of time is called
   - ❏ a. physical fatigue.
   - ❏ b. chronic fatigue.
   - ❏ c. stress fatigue.

4. A common cause of chronic fatigue is
   - ❏ a. obesity.
   - ❏ b. caffeine.
   - ❏ c. exercise.

5. Burnout can result from, among other things,
   - ❏ a. too much rest.
   - ❏ b. lack of organization.
   - ❏ c. a feeling of insecurity.

Understanding Ideas

6. The causes of fatigue are
   - ❏ a. primarily physical.
   - ❏ b. primarily mental.
   - ❏ c. mental and physical.

7. Stressful conditions can cause fatigue
   - ❏ a. in both living and nonliving forms.
   - ❏ b. only in living forms.
   - ❏ c. only in nonliving forms.

8. Fatigue is more likely to occur in
   - ❏ a. very young children.
   - ❏ b. people who are not physically fit.
   - ❏ c. elderly people.

9. You can conclude from the article that endurance limits
   - ❏ a. are greater in men than in women.
   - ❏ b. are the same in all living things.
   - ❏ c. vary from person to person.

10. The relationship of stress to fatigue is one of
    - ❏ a. cause and effect.
    - ❏ b. symptom and disease.
    - ❏ c. approach and avoidance.

9 B   Too Early to Get Up

Brrrring! Brrrring! It's 5:45 A.M. and time for another school day. Christa slaps the alarm into silence. Still half asleep, she showers and pulls on her clothes. Christa is too tired to want breakfast. Besides, she doesn't have time to eat. She has to be at the school bus stop in ten minutes. She bolts down a glass of juice, grabs her books, and rushes out the door.

Christa's first class, chemistry, passes in a daze. The teacher's words don't register. Half the students have their heads down on their desks. Only a few seem able to answer the teacher's questions. After lunch, Christa still feels fatigued, but at least she knows what she's hearing in class. At 2:30, the bell rings, and she hurries off to soccer practice, finally awake.

At dinner, her father asks, "How did your day go?" Christa isn't really sure, but she guesses it went fine. At 10 P.M., her homework finished, she's browsing on her computer. "Go to bed, Chris," her mother calls, but now Christa is wide awake. About 1 A.M., she's finally sleepy. She's in bed by 1:30, asleep as soon as her head hits the pillow. After all, another day begins in only four hours.

1. **Recognizing Words in Context**

   Find the word *register* in the passage. One definition below is a *synonym* for that word; it means the same or almost the same thing. One definition is an *antonym;* it has the opposite or nearly opposite meaning. The other has a completely different meaning. Label the definitions S for *synonym*, A for *antonym*, and D for *different*.

   _____ a. make an impression

   _____ b. enroll

   _____ c. ignore

2. **Distinguishing Fact from Opinion**

   Two of the statements below present *facts*, which can be proved correct. The other statement is an *opinion*, which expresses someone's thoughts or beliefs. Label the statements F for *fact* and O for *opinion*.

   _____ a. Christa's alarm goes off at 5:45 A.M.

   _____ b. Christa should try to get more sleep.

   _____ c. At 2:30, Christa goes to soccer practice.

3. **Keeping Events in Order**

Label the statements below 1, 2, and 3 to show the order in which the events happened.

_____ a. Christa browses on her computer.

_____ b. Christa attends chemistry class.

_____ c. Christa goes to soccer practice.

4. **Making Correct Inferences**

Two of the statements below are correct *inferences,* or reasonable guesses. They are based on information in the passage. The other statement is an incorrect, or faulty, inference. Label the statements C for *correct* inference and F for *faulty* inference.

_____ a. Christa is tired from lack of sleep.

_____ b. Most of the students at Christa's school suffer from fatigue.

_____ c. Being tired makes it difficult to learn.

5. **Understanding Main Ideas**

One of the statements below expresses the main idea of the passage. One statement is too general, or too broad. The other explains only part of the passage; it is too narrow. Label the statements M for *main idea,* B for *too broad,* and N for *too narrow.*

_____ a. Christa's first class passes in a daze.

_____ b. Teenagers get too little sleep.

_____ c. Getting up early and going to bed late causes Christa to be tired and interferes with her education.

Correct Answers, Part A _____

Correct Answers, Part B _____

Total Correct Answers _____

10   A   Euthanasia

Euthanasia generally refers to mercy killing, the voluntary ending of the life of someone who is terminally or hopelessly ill. Euthanasia has become a legal, medical, and ethical issue over which opinion is divided.

Euthanasia can be either active or passive. Active euthanasia means that a physician or other medical personnel takes a deliberate action that will induce death, such as administering an overdose of morphine, insulin, or barbiturates, followed by an injection of curare. Passive euthanasia means letting a patient die for lack of treatment or suspending treatment that has begun. Examples of passive euthanasia include taking patients off a respirator (a breathing apparatus) or removing other life-support systems. Stopping the food supply, usually intravenous feeding, to comatose patients is also considered passive.

A good deal of the controversy about mercy killing stems from the decision-making process. Who decides if a patient is to die? This issue has not been established legally in the United States. The matter is left to state law, which usually allows the physician in charge to suggest the option of death to a patient's relatives, especially if the patient is brain-dead. In an attempt to make decisions about when their own lives should end, some terminally ill patients in the early 1990s used a controversial suicide device, developed by Dr. Jack Kevorkian, to end their lives.

In parts of Europe, the decision-making process has become very flexible. Even in cases in which the patients are not brain-dead, patients have been put to death without their consent at the request of relatives or at the insistence of physicians. Many cases of involuntary euthanasia involve older people or newborn infants. The principle underlying this practice is that such individuals have a "life not worthy of life."

In countries where involuntary euthanasia is not legal, the court systems have proved very lenient in dealing with medical personnel who practice it. Courts have also been somewhat lenient with friends or relatives who have assisted terminally ill patients to die.

Medical advances in recent decades have made it possible to keep terminally ill people alive far beyond any hope of recovery or improvement. For this reason, the "living will" has come into common use in the United States as part of the right-to-die principle. Most states now legally allow the making of such wills that instruct hospitals and physicians to suspend treatment or to refuse life-support measures in hopeless cases.

Reading Time _____

Recalling Facts

1. Active euthanasia is
   - ❏ a. deliberate action to induce death.
   - ❏ b. death caused by accident.
   - ❏ c. the removal of life-support systems.

2. Laws controlling euthanasia are determined by
   - ❏ a. the federal government.
   - ❏ b. each state.
   - ❏ c. the relatives of the patient.

3. An example of passive euthanasia is
   - ❏ a. stopping a patient's food supply.
   - ❏ b. injecting curare.
   - ❏ c. administering an overdose of insulin.

4. Dr. Jack Kevorkian is known for
   - ❏ a. developing the concept of living wills.
   - ❏ b. debating against euthanasia.
   - ❏ c. developing a controversial suicide device.

5. Involuntary euthanasia is legal
   - ❏ a. when a patient's relatives give their consent.
   - ❏ b. in some countries.
   - ❏ c. when medical personnel practice it.

Understanding Ideas

6. You can conclude from the article that people who are against mercy killings
   - ❏ a. are concerned about the rights of patients.
   - ❏ b. feel no sympathy for dying patients.
   - ❏ c. are usually physicians.

7. The issue of euthanasia is apt to be less controversial when a patient
   - ❏ a. is hospitalized.
   - ❏ b. is brain-dead.
   - ❏ c. has no will.

8. Living wills enable patients to
   - ❏ a. avoid terminal illnesses.
   - ❏ b. prolong their lives.
   - ❏ c. make decisions about when their lives should end.

9. You can conclude from the article that the euthanasia controversy in the United States has grown as
   - ❏ a. the population has increased.
   - ❏ b. medical treatment has advanced.
   - ❏ c. physicians have become less competent.

10. The article suggests that the euthanasia issue
    - ❏ a. should be decided by physicians.
    - ❏ b. is primarily a legal issue.
    - ❏ c. is not likely to be easily resolved.

Peter and Buck

"Want to go for a ride, Buck?" Peter knew the old dog could no longer hear much, but he had been talking to him for almost fifteen years. Once a wiggly puppy and then a lively companion, Buck had been failing in the last year. He had developed diabetes. Then he started bumping into things, and the vet said he was going blind. He was in obvious pain when he tried to stand up in the morning. Often Peter had to clean up after him. Old age and illness had ravaged the once strong body. "It's time to think about putting him down," the vet had said.

Peter carried Buck outside and lifted him into the car. Buck had once sat high, ears flapping in the breeze, but now he just lay on the seat. At the vet's, Peter almost picked up his dog and left, but he knew Buck wasn't going to get better. When he was called, Peter carried Buck into the treatment room.

It was over in just a few seconds. A quick injection, and Buck relaxed in Peter's arms. Peter said goodbye to his old friend and left with the now useless collar and leash. He would miss Buck, but he knew he had done the right thing.

1. **Recognizing Words in Context**

   Find the word *failing* in the passage. One definition below is a *synonym* for that word; it means the same or almost the same thing. One definition is an *antonym;* it has the opposite or nearly opposite meaning. The other has a completely different meaning. Label the definitions S for *synonym*, A for *antonym*, and D for *different*.

   _____ a. flunking

   _____ b. weakening

   _____ c. strengthening

2. **Distinguishing Fact from Opinion**

   Two of the statements below present *facts,* which can be proved correct. The other statement is an *opinion,* which expresses someone's thoughts or beliefs. Label the statements F for *fact* and O for *opinion.*

   _____ a. Buck was almost fifteen years old.

   _____ b. It was time to think about putting Buck down.

   _____ c. Buck was almost blind.

3. Keeping Events in Order

Two of the statements below describe events that happened at the same time. The other statement describes an event that happened before or after those events. Label them S for *same time,* B for *before,* and A for *after.*

_____ a. Buck had once sat high in the car.

_____ b. Buck's ears had flapped in the breeze.

_____ c. Buck just lay on the seat.

4. Making Correct Inferences

Two of the statements below are correct *inferences,* or reasonable guesses. They are based on information in the passage. The other statement is an incorrect, or faulty, inference. Label the statements C for *correct* inference and F for *faulty* inference.

_____ a. All old pets should be euthanatized.

_____ b. The injection that the vet gave Buck killed the dog.

_____ c. Euthanatizing a pet is sad for the owner.

5. Understanding Main Ideas

One of the statements below expresses the main idea of the passage. One statement is too general, or too broad. The other explains only part of the passage; it is too narrow. Label the statements M for *main idea,* B for *too broad,* and N for *too narrow.*

_____ a. The vet said it was time to think about putting Buck down.

_____ b. Peter makes the difficult decision to euthanatize his old dog and does so.

_____ c. Euthanasia of hopelessly sick or injured animals is a common practice in the United States.

Correct Answers, Part A _____

Correct Answers, Part B _____

Total Correct Answers _____

Hydroponics

The science of growing plants in water or some substance other than soil is called hydroponics. In hydroponics, or soilless culture, the stems and roots of the plants are supported, and the necessary nutrients for plant growth are provided in the solution surrounding the roots.

All plants need the oxygen, hydrogen, and carbon available from either air or water. They are also dependent on 13 essential elements, the nutrients that are normally acquired from the soil. Some elements, called macronutrients, are taken by plants in large amounts, while in other situations, only trace amounts of elements, or micronutrients, are necessary. The macronutrients are nitrogen, phosphorus, magnesium, sulfur, potassium, and calcium. The micronutrients are iron, chlorine, boron, manganese, zinc, copper, and molybdenum. In hydroponic culture, these chemical elements are supplied to the plants by adding salts that contain them to the solution surrounding the roots.

To begin a hydroponic culture medium, a nutrient solution is prepared in a storage tank by dissolving salt mixtures containing the necessary elements for proper plant growth. Since the plants remove nutrients from the water, the solution is periodically revitalized with the addition of salt mixtures. The acidity level is adjusted. Because of the enormous water uptake by the plants, there is an increase in the sodium-chloride concentration in the water, which is remedied by frequently replenishing the solution in the storage tank.

Although plants may be grown with the roots suspended in a water solution, a variety of other substrates is available. Natural substrates such as gravel, sand, and peat provide support for roots but do not have the nutrients typical of soil. They are used in hydroponic culture with the addition of nutrient-rich solutions. Regardless of the substrate used, the plant roots must be supplied with enough oxygen.

Hydroponics has many advantages over standard soil agricultural practices. Weeds and soil diseases, for example, are not a problem. The area required for a particular crop is considerably reduced because of the greater efficiency of plants at obtaining nutrients directly from the water solution. In addition, crops can be grown in regions where poor soil conditions prevail or in arid climates.

Experimental sites for hydroponic farming exist in regions where poor soils and harsh climates make traditional farming practices inadequate to meet the food requirements of the inhabitants. Major prospects for using hydroponics in agriculture are in arid parts of northern Africa and the Middle East.

Reading Time _____

Recalling Facts

1. Hydroponics is also known as
   - ❏ a. macrobiotics.
   - ❏ b. macronutrients.
   - ❏ c. soilless culture.

2. In addition to 13 essential elements, all plants require
   - ❏ a. soil, air, and water.
   - ❏ b. oxygen, hydrogen, and carbon.
   - ❏ c. gravel, sand, and peat.

3. In a hydroponic culture medium, necessary elements are periodically revitalized by
   - ❏ a. adding salt mixtures to water.
   - ❏ b. increasing sunlight.
   - ❏ c. adding more water.

4. One advantage of hydroponics is
   - ❏ a. plants need fewer nutrients.
   - ❏ b. less attention is required.
   - ❏ c. less room is needed for growing.

5. Plants with roots suspended in a water solution need
   - ❏ a. enough oxygen.
   - ❏ b. additional oxygen.
   - ❏ c. less oxygen.

Understanding Ideas

6. Hydroponic farming is probably
   - ❏ a. the most cost-effective way to farm.
   - ❏ b. a viable solution in areas where traditional farming has proved inadequate.
   - ❏ c. superior to traditional farming.

7. Areas that have harsh climates are most likely
   - ❏ a. ideal for hydroponic farming.
   - ❏ b. inappropriate for hydroponic farming.
   - ❏ c. ideal for traditional farming methods.

8. You can conclude from the article that successful hydroponic farming depends largely on
   - ❏ a. the weather.
   - ❏ b. experimentation.
   - ❏ c. carefully followed scientific procedures.

9. It is likely that hydroponic farming will
   - ❏ a. replace traditional farming in most areas.
   - ❏ b. become more common.
   - ❏ c. remain an experimental program.

10. Hydroponics would be a distinct advantage in areas such as
   - ❏ a. outer space.
   - ❏ b. traditional farming communities in the midwestern United States.
   - ❏ c. New Jersey, known as the "Garden State."

Farmers of the Future

"What are you going to do when you graduate?" Now that they were in high school, Salli's friends had begun seriously asking each other this question. Since grade school, Salli's answer had always been the same: "I'm going to be a farmer."

During the spring of her senior year, Salli worked as an apprentice on the farm that served her district. On her first day, she was tense with excitement as the rapid elevator whisked her to the 130th floor of the building. Salli stepped out into brilliant sunlight. It was coming through the huge glass panes of the greenhouse that covered the acres-wide rooftop. Row upon row of hydroponics tanks stretched out as far as she could see. Each tank was green with plant life.

The farmer who was training Salli walked beside her, explaining the process. He showed her the measuring devices that ensured the plants received the correct mixture of nutrients. One of Salli's tasks would be to monitor these devices.

"Unlike farmers of the past," the farmer told her, "we don't have to worry about weeds, insect pests, and soil-borne diseases. Can you imagine growing food in soil out in the open?"

Salli shuddered at the thought. "Farming used to be so unsanitary!" she exclaimed.

1. **Recognizing Words in Context**

   Find the word *whisked* in the passage. One definition below is a *synonym* for that word; it means the same or almost the same thing. One definition is an *antonym;* it has the opposite or nearly opposite meaning. The other has a completely different meaning. Label the definitions S for *synonym*, A for *antonym*, and D for *different*.

   _____ a. rushed

   _____ b. slowed

   _____ c. stirred

2. **Distinguishing Fact from Opinion**

   Two of the statements below present *facts*, which can be proved correct. The other statement is an *opinion*, which expresses someone's thoughts or beliefs. Label the statements F for *fact* and O for *opinion*.

   _____ a. In the past, farming was unsanitary.

   _____ b. Measuring devices ensured that the plants received the correct mixture of nutrients.

   _____ c. The hydroponics tanks stretched out as far as Salli could see.

3. Keeping Events in Order

Two of the statements below describe events that happened at the same time. The other statement describes an event that happened before or after those events. Label them S for *same time,* B for *before,* and A for *after.*

_____ a. Salli was tense with excitement.

_____ b. Salli stepped out into brilliant sunlight.

_____ c. A rapid elevator carried Salli to the 130th floor.

4. Making Correct Inferences

Two of the statements below are correct *inferences,* or reasonable guesses. They are based on information in the passage. The other statement is an incorrect, or faulty, inference. Label the statements C for *correct* inference and F for *faulty* inference.

_____ a. Weeds, insect pests, and soil-borne diseases have been eliminated from the world.

_____ b. This story takes place in the future.

_____ c. In the time of this story, all farming is done by hydroponics.

5. Understanding Main Ideas

One of the statements below expresses the main idea of the passage. One statement is too general, or too broad. The other explains only part of the passage; it is too narrow. Label the statements M for *main idea,* B for *too broad,* and N for *too narrow.*

_____ a. Salli, who wants to be a farmer, is introduced to the process of hydroponics.

_____ b. Hydroponics is the science of growing plants in water or some substance other than soil.

_____ c. Salli's task would be to monitor the devices that measured the nutrients the plants received.

Correct Answers, Part A _____

Correct Answers, Part B _____

Total Correct Answers _____

Exercise and physical fitness are obviously necessary for athletes, soldiers, fire-fighters, and all those whose jobs require high levels of physical performance. Then why should a sedentary person living in a comfortable, industrialized society exercise?

Medical and health professionals have determined that everyone, depending on the individual's metabolism, has a minimum level of physical activity that must be maintained to prevent serious physical deterioration. The human body and all of its parts, like any living organism, must be used or they atrophy. The loss of structure and function that occurs when a broken arm is immobilized in a cast clearly demonstrates what happens when body parts are not exercised and used.

Basic survival once required the output of enormous physical energy by people on many levels of society. Modern technology has simplified life's physical demands in various ways. Machines from washing machines to automobiles and elaborate industrial equipment have reduced the amount of labor required of people. In more primitive times, most individuals burned up the calories gained from the food they consumed through the rigors of their daily activities. This is no longer true for most people, particularly those living in industrialized nations who do not do strenuous work.

Many people have retained their capacity for physical work. Even those who have been physically inactive for a long time can restore lost physical capability with just a month or two of daily physical training. People who exercise and reach their near-maximum physical capability can maintain it by exercising vigorously on alternate days.

Physical fitness and exercise are important for good physical and mental health, including weight control. Exercise helps the individual develop and maintain a strong self-image and a sense of emotional balance. As a person gets older, exercise becomes more important because after age 30 the heart's blood-pumping capacity declines at a rate of about eight percent every ten years or so.

Most common forms of exercise, such as bicycling and swimming, rarely cause serious injury. But contact sports, such as football and judo, can cause wear on the joints that can lead to articular disease, or joint problems. The problem for most beginners is overexercise. Many people experience stiffness after the first day of exercise, but this is harmless and does not last long. People who are overweight or past middle age or who suffer from heart disease should consult a physician before starting any exercise program.

Reading Time _____

Recalling Facts

1. To stay healthy, everyone should
   - ❑ a. run a mile daily.
   - ❑ b. exercise vigorously twice a week.
   - ❑ c. exercise regularly.

2. If body parts are not used, they will
   - ❑ a. fall off.
   - ❑ b. atrophy.
   - ❑ c. lose their capabilities forever.

3. After age 30, the heart
   - ❑ a. pumps blood more slowly.
   - ❑ b. grows in size.
   - ❑ c. increases its pumping rate.

4. Compared to people in the past, people today generally
   - ❑ a. expend less physical energy on a daily basis.
   - ❑ b. work more strenuously.
   - ❑ c. burn calories faster.

5. Lost physical capability can be restored with
   - ❑ a. two days of exercise.
   - ❑ b. a week of daily physical training.
   - ❑ c. a month or two of daily physical training.

Understanding Ideas

6. Modern technology has resulted in
   - ❑ a. a more simple way of life for most people.
   - ❑ b. less need for strenuous work.
   - ❑ c. an increase in overweight people.

7. People who lead sedentary lives should probably
   - ❑ a. exercise more.
   - ❑ b. work in more physically demanding jobs.
   - ❑ c. lead normal lives.

8. You can conclude from the article that the benefits of exercise are
   - ❑ a. mostly physical.
   - ❑ b. mental as well as physical.
   - ❑ c. experienced mainly by professional athletes.

9. Exercise programs may be dangerous for
   - ❑ a. teenagers.
   - ❑ b. people with fast metabolisms.
   - ❑ c. people with health problems.

10. You can conclude from the article that the potential dangers of physical activity are
    - ❑ a. outweighed by the advantages.
    - ❑ b. not worth the risk.
    - ❑ c. not worthy of consideration.

12   B   Lori Makes a Change

Lori had always been what her grandmother called "pleasingly plump." She insisted that being overweight didn't bother her, but it did. One day, when her study hall desk began to feel uncomfortably snug, Lori decided it was time for a change. Instead of snacking after school, she put on her sweats and took a walk. To her surprise, she came home feeling more energetic than when she went out. At dinner, she turned down second helpings and skipped dessert. The walk seemed to have reduced her appetite.

Lori started walking as much as she could. She packed her own lunches with lots of raw vegetables and volunteered to cook low-fat dinners. Soon her clothes started to feel more comfortable, and the study hall desk wasn't a problem anymore. Friends started to say, "Are you losing weight? You look great!"

Lori knew she would never be willowy and thin like a model, but she was no longer "pleasingly plump." In the spring, she started tennis lessons and joined the hiking club. Now on a hike she no longer feared being the last to reach the top of a hill. Best of all, her doctor said she was healthier than she had ever been.

1. **Recognizing Words in Context**

    Find the word *reduced* in the passage. One definition below is a *synonym* for that word; it means the same or almost the same thing. One definition is an *antonym*; it has the opposite or nearly opposite meaning. The other has a completely different meaning. Label the definitions S for *synonym*, A for *antonym*, and D for *different*.

    _____ a. increased

    _____ b. dieted

    _____ c. lessened

2. **Distinguishing Fact from Opinion**

    Two of the statements below present *facts*, which can be proved correct. The other statement is an *opinion*, which expresses someone's thoughts or beliefs. Label the statements F for *fact* and O for *opinion*.

    _____ a. Her friends said Lori looked great.

    _____ b. Instead of snacking, Lori took a walk.

    _____ c. Lori started tennis lessons in the spring.

3. Keeping Events in Order

Two of the statements below describe events that happened at the same time. The other statement describes an event that happened before or after those events. Label them S for *same time*, B for *before*, and A for *after*.

_____ a. Lori's study hall desk was uncomfortably snug.

_____ b. Lori started walking as much as she could.

_____ c. Lori decided it was time for a change.

4. Making Correct Inferences

Two of the statements below are correct *inferences*, or reasonable guesses. They are based on information in the passage. The other statement is an incorrect, or faulty, inference. Label the statements C for *correct* inference and F for *faulty* inference.

_____ a. Lori made only minor changes to her lifestyle.

_____ b. Before changing her habits, Lori was overweight.

_____ c. Lori's new lifestyle is more active than her previous one.

5. Understanding Main Ideas

One of the statements below expresses the main idea of the passage. One statement is too general, or too broad. The other explains only part of the passage; it is too narrow. Label the statements M for *main idea*, B for *too broad*, and N for *too narrow*.

_____ a. Lori changed her life by changing her fitness habits to include exercise and healthful food choices.

_____ b. A fitness plan can help a person achieve and maintain a healthful weight.

_____ c. Lori decided to change her habits when she could no longer fit comfortably into her study hall desk.

Correct Answers, Part A _____

Correct Answers, Part B _____

Total Correct Answers _____

Podiatric medicine, known as podiatry, is the health profession that cares for the human foot. The doctor of podiatric medicine, called a podiatrist, is responsible for the examination, diagnosis, and treatment of diseases, injuries, and defects of the foot. The condition of the feet can help physicians detect other health problems, including diabetes, various skin diseases, vitamin deficiencies, and vascular problems such as varicose veins in the lower extremities. Podiatry is related to orthopedics, a branch of medicine concerned with correcting problems that involve the bones and joints of the skeletal system.

Podiatry has its roots in early Greek and Roman times and in the fourteenth-century European trade guilds of barber-surgeons. Until the late nineteenth and early twentieth centuries, the practice was known as chiropody. Foot care was limited mainly to the treatment of minor ailments such as corns, bunions, ingrown toenails, and calluses. Practitioners with even a slight amount of skill could claim to be chiropodists. By the mid-1900s, however, the profession had become more organized, particularly in the United States. Practitioners adopted the name *podiatry* to describe their profession, acquired formal training, and used prescription medicines and more sophisticated surgical techniques. In the United States, all podiatrists are required to obtain formal degrees and to be licensed by a qualified board of examiners before they can treat patients.

Nearly 70 percent of the problems handled by podiatrists are inherited. Infants born with malformations of the feet are treated as soon as possible after birth. Treatment includes manipulating the foot into the correct position, placing it in rigid casts or splints, using corrective footwear once the child begins to walk, and, if necessary, correcting problems surgically. Injuries account for only about one-third of the problems podiatrists treat.

Podiatry plays a prominent role in sports medicine, particularly in running sports. To help runners, podiatrists may use orthotic devices. These devices are rigid or semirigid foot supports that hold the foot in the proper position for standing or moving. They relieve stress on the foot and ankle caused by strained or injured tissues, bony prominences, deformed bones, torn or stretched ligaments, and even some skin disorders.

Podiatrists may specialize in one of several areas within podiatric medicine, including dermatology, sports medicine, foot problems of children, treatment of the elderly, corrective surgery, and radiology. Podiatric specialists may not limit their practice to their specialties but may engage in general podiatry as well.

Reading Time _____

Recalling Facts

1. The health profession that cares for the human foot is called
   - ❏ a. pediatrics.
   - ❏ b. podiatry.
   - ❏ c. psychiatry.

2. Before the late nineteenth century, foot doctors were called
   - ❏ a. chiropodists.
   - ❏ b. podiatrists.
   - ❏ c. surgeons.

3. Podiatric medicine dates back to
   - ❏ a. twelfth-century China.
   - ❏ b. early Greek and Roman times.
   - ❏ c. sixteenth-century Europe.

4. Most of the problems handled by foot doctors today are
   - ❏ a. caused by accidents.
   - ❏ b. the result of poor health care.
   - ❏ c. inherited.

5. Foot supports are called
   - ❏ a. sports aids.
   - ❏ b. orthotic devices.
   - ❏ c. shoe splints.

Understanding Ideas

6. You can conclude from the article that the field of foot care has become
   - ❏ a. more professional.
   - ❏ b. too specialized.
   - ❏ c. less formal.

7. The article suggests that foot problems
   - ❏ a. are usually related to other health problems.
   - ❏ b. are rarely inherited.
   - ❏ c. may be related to other health problems.

8. It is likely that early foot-care specialists
   - ❏ a. had little formal training.
   - ❏ b. were well organized.
   - ❏ c. dealt with total body health.

9. The article suggests that inherited foot problems are best treated
   - ❏ a. surgically.
   - ❏ b. after the feet are fully formed.
   - ❏ c. as soon as possible after birth.

10. You can conclude from the article that standards for foot care in the United States are
    - ❏ a. stringent.
    - ❏ b. too restrictive.
    - ❏ c. lax.

13 B   Jorge's Problem

Jorge was one of the fastest runners on the high school track team. Then his feet and ankles began to hurt whenever he ran. He didn't tell anyone about the problem, because he didn't want to seem like a wimp. However, the pain was affecting his performance on the track.

The track coach finally took Jorge aside and asked, "What's wrong, Jorge? You're not running the way you used to."

"You're not going to drop me from the team, are you, Coach?" Jorge asked nervously.

"I just want to help," the coach replied. Jorge explained about the pain he had been feeling in his feet and ankles when he ran.

"This sounds like something a doctor needs to look into, Jorge," the coach told him.

Jorge's family doctor referred him to a podiatrist. The podiatrist watched Jorge walk and run on a treadmill. "I think we can correct this problem," she told him.

"Will I be able to run fast again?" Jorge asked.

"You'll be at the head of the pack again in no time!" she assured him. She created devices for Jorge to wear in his running shoes that held his feet in the proper position. Soon the pain was gone, and Jorge was running fast races again.

1. **Recognizing Words in Context**

    Find the word *wrong* in the passage. One definition below is a *synonym* for that word; it means the same or almost the same thing. One definition is an *antonym*; it has the opposite or nearly opposite meaning. The other has a completely different meaning. Label the definitions S for *synonym*, A for *antonym*, and D for *different*.

    _____ a. unsatisfactory

    _____ b. acceptable

    _____ c. incorrect

2. **Distinguishing Fact from Opinion**

    Two of the statements below present *facts*, which can be proved correct. The other statement is an *opinion*, which expresses someone's thoughts or beliefs. Label the statements F for *fact* and O for *opinion*.

    _____ a. Jorge began to feel pain in his feet and ankles when he ran.

    _____ b. The podiatrist watched Jorge walk and run on a treadmill.

    _____ c. Jorge would be at the head of the pack in no time.

3. Keeping Events in Order

Label the statements below 1, 2, and 3 to show the order in which the events happened.

_____ a. Jorge went to see a podiatrist.

_____ b. Jorge's coach asked him what was wrong.

_____ c. Jorge wore devices in his running shoes that held his feet in the proper position.

4. Making Correct Inferences

Two of the statements below are correct *inferences*, or reasonable guesses. They are based on information in the passage. The other statement is an incorrect, or faulty, inference. Label the statements C for *correct* inference and F for *faulty* inference.

_____ a. Because of the pain, Jorge was not running as well as he used to.

_____ b. All foot problems can be corrected with devices worn in a person's shoes.

_____ c. Jorge's problem was caused by improper foot position when he ran.

5. Understanding Main Ideas

One of the statements below expresses the main idea of the passage. One statement is too general, or too broad. The other explains only part of the passage; it is too narrow. Label the statements M for *main idea*, B for *too broad*, and N for *too narrow*.

_____ a. Podiatric medicine, known as podiatry, is the health profession that cares for the human foot.

_____ b. A podiatrist created devices for Jorge to wear in his running shoes that held his feet in the proper position.

_____ c. Jorge, a member of the track team, developed foot problems that affected his ability to run but that a podiatrist was able to correct.

Correct Answers, Part A _____

Correct Answers, Part B _____

Total Correct Answers _____

A social science rather than a branch of law, criminology deals with the causes, correction, and prevention of criminal behavior. Although it is a specialty, it is not a single discipline. It combines the efforts of statisticians, psychiatrists, sociologists, lawyers, police officials, probation officers, and most recently biologists.

Whereas traditional legal approaches to crime focus on the criminal act and the protection of society, criminology centers its attention on the criminal as a person, the criminal's behavior, and what has led the person to a life of crime. It seeks to understand the criminal's genetic makeup to learn whether there is an inherited tendency to crime. It also takes into consideration such issues as the individual's socioeconomic background, family upbringing, educational opportunities, and childhood associations.

A major interest of criminologists is correction. What should be done with the criminal once caught, tried, and convicted? Until the late nineteenth century, penalties consisted primarily of public humiliation, beatings or torture, banishment or exile, death, fines, or confiscation of property. Imprisonment as a penalty became common after the sixteenth century but only for lesser offenses.

Not until the late nineteenth century did imprisonment become the most common penalty for most crimes. Gradually, the purpose of imprisonment began to shift from confinement to attempts to turn prisoners away from the life of crime when they were released. Prisons for young offenders were called reformatories; they gave greater emphasis to education for their inmates.

Probably the most significant developments have been probation and parole. Under probation, the sentence of a convicted criminal is suspended if the criminal promises to behave well, accept some supervision of his or her life, and meet certain requirements. Parole involves conditional release from confinement after part of a sentence has already been served. It is granted if the prisoner seems to have changed into an honest and trustworthy person.

In the second half of the twentieth century, work-release programs and halfway houses were established. In a work-release program, offenders are released from prison for part of each day to work at an outside job or to attend school. Halfway houses are establishments to help former prisoners readjust to the outside world after completion of a prison sentence.

The uses of imprisonment, probation, parole, halfway houses, and work-release programs have been closely studied by criminologists to learn which means are most effective in reforming criminals and in guiding them to productive lives.

Reading Time _____

Recalling Facts

1. Criminology is a
   - ❏ a. branch of law.
   - ❏ b. social science.
   - ❏ c. correctional system.

2. After the late nineteenth century, the most common penalty for crimes was
   - ❏ a. public humiliation.
   - ❏ b. fines.
   - ❏ c. imprisonment.

3. Emphasis in reformatories for young offenders was on
   - ❏ a. confinement.
   - ❏ b. punishment.
   - ❏ c. education.

4. Release from confinement after part of a sentence has been served is called
   - ❏ a. parole.
   - ❏ b. probation.
   - ❏ c. reformation.

5. Halfway houses are establishments that
   - ❏ a. help society adjust to a prisoner.
   - ❏ b. help former prisoners readjust to the outside world.
   - ❏ c. protect society from former prisoners.

Understanding Ideas

6. Criminology, unlike traditional legal approaches to crime, has its basis in
   - ❏ a. the psychology of the individual.
   - ❏ b. legal procedures.
   - ❏ c. economic issues.

7. You can conclude from the article that the approach to criminal behavior has become more
   - ❏ a. insensitive.
   - ❏ b. sympathetic.
   - ❏ c. monotonous.

8. Developments in criminology assume that criminals
   - ❏ a. have inherited a tendency to crime.
   - ❏ b. should remain in prison for the protection of society.
   - ❏ c. have the capacity to change for the better.

9. The concept of work-release programs is to
   - ❏ a. penalize criminals for their behavior.
   - ❏ b. help offenders become useful members of society.
   - ❏ c. tempt offenders to be dishonest.

10. Contemporary criminology assumes that educated criminals
   - ❏ a. are less likely to return to prison.
   - ❏ b. will most likely return to prison.
   - ❏ c. will become teachers in the outside world.

14　B　　　How Criminology Developed

In 1764, Cesare Beccaria, an Italian, published *Essays on Crime and Punishment*. His book was the first attempt to apply principles of logic to crime, and eventually it led to the science of criminology.

Over the next hundred years, cities grew and police forces developed. Better record keeping meant that people could more easily study what kinds of crimes were committed and by whom. But no effort was made to discover why people committed crimes or to delve into the criminal mind.

In 1876, another Italian, Cesare Lombroso, published a work describing a "criminal type." Lombroso concluded that some people were "born criminals." At first, his ideas had wide appeal, but they were later disproved. People began to look more at the social environment from which criminals came.

In the twentieth century, criminologists began scrutinizing the influences that cause people to become criminals, using both case studies and crime figures. From being a simple study of crime itself, criminology evolved into an exploration of the reasons for crime and the relationship of crime to society as a whole. Students of criminology find work in law enforcement, government, prisons, and parole and probation agencies as well as in colleges and universities.

1. **Recognizing Words in Context**

   Find the word *scrutinizing* in the passage. One definition below is a *synonym* for that word; it means the same or almost the same thing. One definition is an *antonym*; it has the opposite or nearly opposite meaning. The other has a completely different meaning. Label the definitions S for *synonym*, A for *antonym*, and D for *different*.

   _____ a. ignoring

   _____ b. examining closely

   _____ c. wondering about

2. **Distinguishing Fact from Opinion**

   Two of the statements below present *facts*, which can be proved correct. The other statement is an *opinion*, which expresses someone's thoughts or beliefs. Label the statements F for *fact* and O for *opinion*.

   _____ a. Cesare Beccaria was the first to apply logic to the study of crime.

   _____ b. Cesare Lombroso described a "criminal type" in 1876.

   _____ c. Lombroso's ideas had wide appeal.

3. **Keeping Events in Order**

   Label the statements below 1, 2, and 3 to show the order in which the events happened.

   _____ a. Cesare Beccaria published *Essays on Crime and Punishment.*

   _____ b. The theory of a "criminal type" was disproved.

   _____ c. Researchers began studying why people become criminals.

4. **Making Correct Inferences**

   Two of the statements below are correct *inferences,* or reasonable guesses. They are based on information in the passage. The other statement is an incorrect, or faulty, inference. Label the statements C for *correct* inference and F for *faulty* inference.

   _____ a. The focus of criminology has changed greatly since its beginnings.

   _____ b. Crime was simpler in 1764.

   _____ c. Criminology is meant to help stop crime.

5. **Understanding Main Ideas**

   One of the statements below expresses the main idea of the passage. One statement is too general, or too broad. The other explains only part of the passage; it is too narrow. Label the statements M for *main idea,* B for *too broad,* and N for *too narrow.*

   _____ a. Criminology is the study of crime.

   _____ b. Better record keeping in the nineteenth century meant that people could more easily study crime and criminals.

   _____ c. In its development as a science, criminology has moved from knowing about crimes toward understanding why people commit them.

   Correct Answers, Part A _____

   Correct Answers, Part B _____

   Total Correct Answers _____

15　A　Juvenile Courts

The purpose of juvenile courts is to establish and supervise a plan of control and rehabilitation for youths who have broken the laws of their community. Most juvenile courts are also responsible for legal matters involving dependent and neglected children.

The largest number of juvenile court cases involves juvenile delinquency. A juvenile court has traditionally regarded young offenders (usually through age 17) as those who are in trouble because they are in situations beyond their control. Regardless of the offense, such a program is devised to reestablish young offenders as good citizens of the community. Experience has shown that in dealing with young people under these circumstances the best results are achieved when the courts operate without a trial atmosphere.

After the original complaint and arrest, a judge and the judge's staff take over. The staff, which frequently includes psychologists, psychiatrists, social workers, and other specially trained workers, investigates the situation and the offender. On the basis of what is found, the judge and the staff establish and carry out a plan of rehabilitation, which may involve a period of residence in a corrective institution, medical treatment, a foster home for the youth, probation (continued supervision by the court), or any other corrective plan that seems desirable.

By the late 1980s, alternative sentencing included community service, making amends to victims, and paramilitary discipline (short-term incarceration in special sections of state prisons). Increased parental liability is another trend for such offenses as allowing a child to participate in a gang, to be truant from school, to use drugs, or to have access to a gun; punishments for the parents range from fines to eviction from public housing to imprisonment.

While parental accountability has increased, so has the tendency to try as adults those youths who have committed serious crimes. In 1989, the United States Supreme Court ruled that the Constitution does not forbid the death penalty for those who commit murder at age 16 or 17.

In 1869, Boston started separate sessions of court for juvenile offenders. The first court to hear cases and deliver sentences solely for children, however, was established in 1899 in Chicago. The Boston juvenile court was established in 1906, and the next year, Denver opened its juvenile court.

Juvenile courts now exist in most of the United States, Europe, and Latin America, as well as Israel, Japan, and other countries, though structure and procedure vary.

Reading Time _____

Recalling Facts

1. The largest number of juvenile court cases involves
   - ❏ a. juvenile delinquency.
   - ❏ b. car theft.
   - ❏ c. serious crimes.

2. Juvenile courts deal with offenders
   - ❏ a. under the age of 21.
   - ❏ b. aged 17 and under.
   - ❏ c. aged 12 and under.

3. Released offenders requiring continued supervision by the court are put
   - ❏ a. in foster homes.
   - ❏ b. in jail.
   - ❏ c. on probation.

4. Punishment for offenses such as juvenile drug use or truancy
   - ❏ a. may include life in jail.
   - ❏ b. may be given to the parents of the offender.
   - ❏ c. often involves community service.

5. Youths who have committed murder
   - ❏ a. may be tried as adults.
   - ❏ b. are treated as juvenile delinquents.
   - ❏ c. are sentenced to short-term incarceration.

Understanding Ideas

6. Juvenile court is based on the idea that
   - ❏ a. young offenders can be rehabilitated.
   - ❏ b. young people don't know right from wrong.
   - ❏ c. forgiveness is more effective than punishment.

7. You can conclude from the article that the court system believes that juvenile offenders
   - ❏ a. should be treated the same as adults.
   - ❏ b. should be treated differently from adults.
   - ❏ c. are more likely to be rehabilitated than adults.

8. Juvenile court recognizes that parents of offenders
   - ❏ a. deserve to be punished.
   - ❏ b. are guilty of child neglect.
   - ❏ c. share the responsibility for a child's offenses.

9. Juvenile courts are widespread, which suggests that
   - ❏ a. they achieve good results.
   - ❏ b. crime doesn't pay.
   - ❏ c. most juvenile offenders are rehabilitated.

10. You can conclude from the article that juvenile delinquency is
    - ❏ a. a problem mainly in the United States.
    - ❏ b. a worldwide problem.
    - ❏ c. increasing.

Mark Tully stood before the judge's bench with his head bowed. Beside Mark, his lawyer was telling the judge about Mark's lack of a criminal record and his high grades in school. The judge leaned toward Mark.

"Young man, are you denying that you stole the video game?" she asked.

"No, ma'am," Mark mumbled, eyes on the floor.

"Can you tell me why you took it?"

"A dare," Mark said softly.

"Look at me when you answer, Mr. Tully!" the judge commanded. "Did I hear you say 'dare'?"

Mark looked at the judge pleadingly. "Yes, ma'am. My friends said I was chicken if I didn't lift the game. I didn't want the guys to drop me!"

"Do you think that real friends would base their friendship on whether or not you stole something?"

"I guess not, ma'am," Mark mumbled.

"Do you think that what you did was right?"

"No, ma'am! I know it was wrong," Mark said more firmly.

The judge looked at Mark thoughtfully. "I sentence you to six months' probation," she said at last. "I'm releasing you to the custody of your parents. I hope you've learned a lesson from this."

"I have, ma'am!" Mark said with relief.

1. Recognizing Words in Context

Find the word *dare* in the passage. One definition below is a *synonym* for that word; it means the same or almost the same thing. One definition is an *antonym;* it has the opposite or nearly opposite meaning. The other has a completely different meaning. Label the definitions S for *synonym*, A for *antonym*, and D for *different*.

_____ a. challenge

_____ b. defy

_____ c. easy task

2. Distinguishing Fact from Opinion

Two of the statements below present *facts*, which can be proved correct. The other statement is an *opinion*, which expresses someone's thoughts or beliefs. Label the statements F for *fact* and O for *opinion*.

_____ a. Mark admitted to having stolen a video game.

_____ b. Mark's friends had dared him to steal the game.

_____ c. The judge should have given Mark a harsher sentence than probation.

3. Keeping Events in Order

Two of the statements below describe events that happened at the same time. The other statement describes an event that happened before or after those events. Label them S for *same time,* B for *before,* and A for *after.*

_____ a. Mark's lawyer told the judge that Mark had no criminal record.

_____ b. Mark stood in front of the judge with his head bowed.

_____ c. The judge told Mark to look at her when he spoke.

4. Making Correct Inferences

Two of the statements below are correct *inferences,* or reasonable guesses. They are based on information in the passage. The other statement is an incorrect, or faulty, inference. Label the statements C for *correct* inference and F for *faulty* inference.

_____ a. The judge did not think that Mark was really a criminal.

_____ b. Mark would not have stolen the video game if his friends had not dared him to do so.

_____ c. Mark still values the friendship of the boys who dared him to steal the video game.

5. Understanding Main Ideas

One of the statements below expresses the main idea of the passage. One statement is too general, or too broad. The other explains only part of the passage; it is too narrow. Label the statements M for *main idea,* B for *too broad,* and N for *too narrow.*

_____ a. The judge released Mark Tully into the custody of his parents.

_____ b. It is the duty of a juvenile court judge to determine the most appropriate sentence for an offender.

_____ c. Having confessed to stealing a video game on a dare, Mark Tully is sentenced to six months' probation.

Correct Answers, Part A _____

Correct Answers, Part B _____

Total Correct Answers _____

16 A   Malnutrition

Any disorder of nutrition, whether it is due to dietary deficiency, called undernutrition, or to excess, called overnutrition, is known as malnutrition. Malnutrition can be caused by insufficient food intake, an unbalanced diet, or a defect in how the body processes food.

Malnutrition often results from a shortage of calories, protein, vitamins, or minerals; it can also result from a paucity of any combination of these. Deficiencies of protein and calories usually occur together, and because protein is essential for growth, such protein-calorie malnutrition can have serious effects on children, including mental retardation.

Vitamin and mineral deficiencies can result in a range of health problems. For instance, vitamin C deficiency, or scurvy, produces abnormal bone growth in infants; in adults it results in swollen and bleeding gums, loosened teeth, joint stiffness, and anemia. Vitamin A deficiency leads to night blindness and other sight disorders. Calcium deficiency inhibits the formation of bones and teeth in children. Loss of taste and smell can result from zinc deficiency, and iodine deficiency causes goiter, or enlargement of the thyroid gland.

In developed nations, obesity is the most common form of malnutrition. Corpulence can lead to diabetes and hormonal disturbances and can also contribute to heart, kidney, and circulatory diseases.

Overnutrition, or the ingestion of excessive amounts of nutrients, can result in health problems that are just as serious as those caused by vitamin and mineral deficiencies. For example, an excess of animal fat in the diet can cause high cholesterol levels, which may lead to circulatory disease, and toxic levels of vitamins A and D cause acute illness.

The primary cause of malnutrition in industrialized nations is economic deprivation, or the inability to afford necessary foods. Poor eating habits also play a role. The elderly often develop poor eating habits because of ill health, depression, or limited income. Nutritional imbalance can occur as a result of fad diets and appetite-suppressing drugs. Emotional disorders, especially depression and anorexia nervosa, can lead to serious nutritional problems. A variety of nutritional disorders, particularly thiamine deficiencies, are common among alcoholics.

In developing nations, the unavailability of food is the primary cause of malnutrition. Famine, war, and unreliable systems of food distribution contribute to the ongoing problem of world hunger.

Agencies such as the World Health Organization have been formed to combat world hunger. Their efforts range from supplying food during emergencies to teaching sound agricultural practices in developing countries.

Reading Time _____

Recalling Facts

1. One cause of malnutrition is
   - ❏ a. an unbalanced diet.
   - ❏ b. loss of taste.
   - ❏ c. aging.

2. Vitamin C deficiency leads to
   - ❏ a. anemia.
   - ❏ b. sight disorders.
   - ❏ c. goiter.

3. Overnutrition is
   - ❏ a. the ingestion of food high in cholesterol.
   - ❏ b. the loss of vitamins and minerals.
   - ❏ c. the ingestion of excessive amounts of nutrients.

4. The primary cause of malnutrition in industrialized nations is
   - ❏ a. alcoholism.
   - ❏ b. economic deprivation.
   - ❏ c. ill health.

5. The unavailability of food is the primary cause of malnutrition in
   - ❏ a. developed nations.
   - ❏ b. developing nations.
   - ❏ c. the Northern Hemisphere.

Understanding Ideas

6. The cause of malnutrition is probably most commonly thought to be
   - ❏ a. a lack of food.
   - ❏ b. too much food.
   - ❏ c. poorly cooked food.

7. It is likely that a child with poor bone and teeth formation suffers from
   - ❏ a. obesity.
   - ❏ b. high cholesterol.
   - ❏ c. a mineral deficiency.

8. A person whose body cannot process food properly is probably
   - ❏ a. malnourished.
   - ❏ b. too thin.
   - ❏ c. too heavy.

9. Victims of malnutrition in the United States are most likely to be
   - ❏ a. wealthy.
   - ❏ b. poor.
   - ❏ c. alcoholics.

10. The article suggests that world hunger
    - ❏ a. is no longer a problem.
    - ❏ b. can be solved easily.
    - ❏ c. is a serious problem.

The Cure for Scurvy

Until the end of the eighteenth century, sailors on long sea voyages often developed mysterious symptoms. Their gums bled, and their teeth loosened and fell out. Their joints ached. They bruised easily, and injuries would not heal. The sailors were often too weak to work. Their illness, called scurvy, had been known for centuries, but its cause was unknown.

In 1749, a Scottish naval doctor named James Lind proved that scurvy was caused by the lack of fresh fruits and vegetables in the sailors' diet. Lind's experiments showed that adding citrus fruit to the sailors' diet both cured and prevented scurvy. Lind announced his findings in 1753. It was not until 1795, however, that the British navy began issuing lime juice to all its sailors at sea. Some people made fun of this practice and started calling British sailors "limeys." It was no laughing matter—scurvy disappeared on board British ships. In 1854, Parliament enacted a law requiring merchant ships to issue lime juice to their crews.

Today we know that the sailors with scurvy suffered from a deficiency of vitamin C—a vitamin that must be consumed every day to be effective. Lime juice, rich in vitamin C, helped make the British navy one of the strongest fighting forces in the world.

1. Recognizing Words in Context

Find the word *consumed* in the passage. One definition below is a *synonym* for that word; it means the same or almost the same thing. One definition is an *antonym*; it has the opposite or nearly opposite meaning. The other has a completely different meaning. Label the definitions S for *synonym*, A for *antonym*, and D for *different*.

_____ a. ingested

_____ b. destroyed

_____ c. ejected

2. Distinguishing Fact from Opinion

Two of the statements below present *facts*, which can be proved correct. The other statement is an *opinion*, which expresses someone's thoughts or beliefs. Label the statements F for *fact* and O for *opinion*.

_____ a. A Scottish doctor named James Lind discovered the cause of scurvy.

_____ b. Making sailors drink lime juice was amusing.

_____ c. Scurvy disappeared on board British ships after sailors were given lime juice.

3. Keeping Events in Order

Label the statements below 1, 2, and 3 to show the order in which the events happened.

_____ a. The British navy began giving its sailors lime juice.

_____ b. Parliament required merchant ships to give their crews lime juice.

_____ c. James Lind discovered the cause of scurvy.

4. Making Correct Inferences

Two of the statements below are correct *inferences,* or reasonable guesses. They are based on information in the passage. The other statement is an incorrect, or faulty, inference. Label the statements C for *correct* inference and F for *faulty* inference.

_____ a. Lime juice was easier to carry on ships than fresh fruits and vegetables.

_____ b. Long sea voyages created perfect conditions for scurvy.

_____ c. Scurvy was unavoidable on long voyages.

5. Understanding Main Ideas

One of the statements below expresses the main idea of the passage. One statement is too general, or too broad. The other explains only part of the passage; it is too narrow. Label the statements M for *main idea,* B for *too broad,* and N for *too narrow.*

_____ a. Until the late eighteenth century, sailors on long sea voyages often suffered from scurvy.

_____ b. Fresh fruits and vegetables are an important part of a healthful diet.

_____ c. After James Lind proved in 1749 that citrus fruits can cure scurvy, the British navy began issuing lime juice to its sailors, wiping out the disease on its ships.

Correct Answers, Part A _____

Correct Answers, Part B _____

Total Correct Answers _____

The oil used to heat homes and businesses, the water used for drinking and bathing, and the gasoline used for fuel are all made available by way of pipelines. Pipelines are lines of pipe equipped with pumps, valves, and other control devices for transporting materials from their remote sources to storage tanks or refineries and, in turn, to distribution facilities. They may also carry industrial waste and sewage to processing plants for treatment and disposal.

Pipelines vary in diameter from the 2-inch (5-centimeter) lines used in oil-well gathering systems to lines 30 feet (9 meters) across used in high-volume water and sewage networks. Pipelines usually consist of sections of pipe made of steel, cast iron, or aluminum, though some are constructed of concrete, clay products, and occasionally plastics. The joined sections are laid underground.

Because such great quantities of often expensive and sometimes environmentally harmful material are carried through pipelines, it is essential that the systems be well constructed and monitored in order to ensure that they will operate smoothly, efficiently, and safely. The pipes are often covered with a protective coating of coal-tar enamel, asphalt, or plastic. These coatings may be reinforced by a sheath of asbestos felt, fiberglass, or polyurethane. The materials used depend on the substance to be carried and its chemical activity and possible corrosive action on the pipe. Pipeline designers must also consider such factors as the capacity of the pipeline, internal and external pressures affecting the pipeline, water- and airtightness, and construction and operating costs.

Generally, the first step in construction is to dig a trench deep enough to allow for approximately 20 inches (51 centimeters) of soil to cover the pipe. Sections of pipe, usually about 40 feet (12 meters) long, are then held over the trench, where they are joined together, covered with a protective coating, and lowered into position. The sections may be joined by welding, riveting, or mechanical coupling.

The pipelines of some water-supply systems may follow the slope of the land, winding through irregular landscapes as railroads and highways do, and rely on gravity to keep the water flowing through them. If necessary, the gravity flow is supplemented by pumping. Most pipelines, however, are operated under pressure to overcome friction within the pipe and differences in elevation. Such systems have a series of pumping stations that are located at intervals of from 50 to 200 miles (80 to 322 kilometers).

Reading Time _____

Recalling Facts

1. Pipelines used in high-volume water networks can be
   - ❑ a. 10 feet (3 meters) across.
   - ❑ b. 20 feet (6 meters) across.
   - ❑ c. 30 feet (9 meters) across.

2. Pipelines are usually made of
   - ❑ a. metal.
   - ❑ b. clay.
   - ❑ c. concrete.

3. Among other things, pipeline designers are concerned with
   - ❑ a. the cost of copper.
   - ❑ b. operating costs.
   - ❑ c. farming methods.

4. To make use of gravity, some pipelines are built to
   - ❑ a. run uphill.
   - ❑ b. follow the slope of the land.
   - ❑ c. bend every few feet.

5. Most pipelines have a pumping station
   - ❑ a. every 50 to 200 miles (80 to 322 kilometers).
   - ❑ b. every 150 to 300 miles (241 to 483 kilometers).
   - ❑ c. every 15 to 50 miles (24 to 80 kilometers).

Understanding Ideas

6. The article suggests that one problem with pipelines is
   - ❑ a. controlling pipe length.
   - ❑ b. maintaining the flow of materials.
   - ❑ c. obtaining materials for construction.

7. You can conclude from the article that pipes carrying harmful materials
   - ❑ a. are reinforced.
   - ❑ b. are longer than average.
   - ❑ c. do not have coatings.

8. Pipes in large cities are likely to be
   - ❑ a. large in diameter.
   - ❑ b. small in diameter.
   - ❑ c. average in diameter.

9. The article wants you to understand that pipeline construction is
   - ❑ a. becoming obsolete.
   - ❑ b. a simple process.
   - ❑ c. a job for experts.

10. The deeper a pipeline is buried, the
    - ❑ a. more it is affected by gravity.
    - ❑ b. sooner it needs repair.
    - ❑ c. more time-consuming it is to repair.

The Trans-Alaska Pipeline

Shrouded in a heavy, fur-trimmed parka, Mike Kelleher worked the levers of his backhoe, hacking a load of soil out of the frozen tundra. The temperature was –70°F (–57°C), and at that low temperature, metal becomes brittle and can break easily. Mike was careful not to put too much strain on his machine as he dropped his load and went back for another.

The 14-foot-deep (4.3-meter-deep) trench Mike was digging would house a section of the trans-Alaska pipeline. Buried safely below the permafrost, the pipeline would transport oil a distance of 800 miles (1,287 kilometers) from the rich oil fields of Prudhoe Bay on Alaska's frozen Arctic coast to the ice-free waters of Valdez on the southern coast. From there, tankers would carry the oil to refineries.

Mike was just one of some 20,000 workers battling harsh weather and Alaska's challenging terrain to construct the pipeline. Work had begun in 1973. The line crossed mountains as high as 4,800 feet (1,463 meters), as well as 34 major rivers and streams. Blizzards halted work during the long, dark winter. Equipment broke down in the cold. Workers quit under the strain. But oil flowed through the completed pipeline in 1977.

1. Recognizing Words in Context

Find the word *coast* in the passage. One definition below is a *synonym* for that word; it means the same or almost the same thing. One definition is an *antonym;* it has the opposite or nearly opposite meaning. The other has a completely different meaning. Label the definitions S for *synonym*, A for *antonym*, and D for *different*.

_____ a. interior

_____ b. shoreline

_____ c. slide

2. Distinguishing Fact from Opinion

Two of the statements below present *facts*, which can be proved correct. The other statement is an *opinion*, which expresses someone's thoughts or beliefs. Label the statements F for *fact* and O for *opinion*.

_____ a. Pipeline workers were a tough bunch of people.

_____ b. The trans-Alaska pipeline was completed in 1977.

_____ c. Sections of pipe were buried 14 feet (4.3 meters) underground.

3. Keeping Events in Order

Label the statements below 1, 2, and 3 to show the order in which the events happened.

_____ a. Oil flowed through the pipeline in 1977.

_____ b. Some 20,000 workers labored to construct the pipeline.

_____ c. Work on the pipeline began in 1973.

4. Making Correct Inferences

Two of the statements below are correct *inferences,* or reasonable guesses. They are based on information in the passage. The other statement is an incorrect, or faulty, inference. Label the statements C for *correct* inference and F for *faulty* inference.

_____ a. Work on the pipeline stopped for the entire winter.

_____ b. The building of the pipeline was a huge undertaking.

_____ c. Alaska's weather created major problems for the pipeline workers.

5. Understanding Main Ideas

One of the statements below expresses the main idea of the passage. One statement is too general, or too broad. The other explains only part of the passage; it is too narrow. Label the statements M for *main idea*, B for *too broad*, and N for *too narrow*.

_____ a. From 1973 to 1977, some 20,000 people worked to build an oil pipeline 800 miles (1,287 kilometers) long across Alaska.

_____ b. Sections of the pipeline were buried in a 14-foot-deep (4.3-meter-deep) trench.

_____ c. The demand for energy in the forms of oil and natural gas has created a wave of pipeline construction around the world.

Correct Answers, Part A _____

Correct Answers, Part B _____

Total Correct Answers _____

18   A   Industrial Medicine

From at least the time of the early Egyptians, physicians noticed that health could be damaged in certain occupations. Lead and mercury miners died of poisoning, and stonecutters suffered severe breathing problems. The goal of modern industrial medicine, the branch of medicine dealing with work-related health problems, is to contribute to the health of workers and to assure that the work environment is as free of hazards as possible.

By 1920, most industrial countries had protective laws and gave workers money as compensation if they became too sick to work. However, the problem of job hazards continues because of the increasing use of radioactive materials and caustic chemicals.

The most widespread job hazards encountered today are harmful dusts. Many coal miners are subject to permanent lung damage from coal dust. Textile workers contract it from cotton dust, and potters, granite workers, and sandblasters from the silica in sand and quartz. Dust from asbestos, a silica compound, can lead to an especially severe lung impairment and cancer. Organic dusts from grain, fur, feathers, and molds cause asthma and other allergies in many workers.

Lead and mercury poisoning remain problems, causing nervous system disorders from headaches to tremors to paralysis. Among the hazardous industrial metals are cadmium, used in metal plating and batteries, and beryllium, used in electronics and aerospace industries, both of which affect lungs and other organs.

To the physically challenging work environments that traditionally carry a burden of ill health—extreme heat or cold, dampness, and the high-pressure atmospheres faced by divers and tunnel workers—have been added such modern threats as deafening noise levels and penetrating radiation. Especially troublesome are the highly poisonous halogenated hydrocarbons—compounds containing hydrogen and carbon in combination with chlorine, fluorine, bromine, or iodine. Most are irritating to all living tissue on contact; many attack the nervous system or cause liver damage, cancer, reproductive disorders, and a host of other problems.

In offices, the hazards of indoor pollution are being recognized as the cause of such health problems as headaches, fatigue, breathing difficulties, and dizziness. Indoor pollutants include cigarette smoke, chemicals used in copy materials, and stale air from poor ventilation systems.

Modern industrial medicine also takes account of workers' individual problems both in the manufacturing trades and the service and communications sectors. Stress, alcoholism and other drug abuse, and time-shift fatigue are some personal factors that can undermine health and contribute to accidents.

Reading Time _____

Recalling Facts

1. Industrial medicine deals with
   - ❏ a. work-related health problems.
   - ❏ b. problems in the natural environment.
   - ❏ c. problems with machinery.

2. The most widespread job hazards today are
   - ❏ a. high temperatures.
   - ❏ b. lack of water.
   - ❏ c. harmful dusts.

3. Hazardous industrial metals include
   - ❏ a. quartz.
   - ❏ b. radioactive materials.
   - ❏ c. lead and mercury.

4. Indoor pollutants in offices include
   - ❏ a. stale air.
   - ❏ b. high noise levels.
   - ❏ c. penetrating radiation.

5. Personal factors that can undermine the health of workers are
   - ❏ a. stress and drug abuse.
   - ❏ b. poor weather conditions.
   - ❏ c. paid vacations.

Understanding Ideas

6. The article suggests that job hazards
   - ❏ a. are easy to control.
   - ❏ b. cannot be controlled.
   - ❏ c. can be controlled.

7. You can conclude from the article that job-related health problems
   - ❏ a. are a new issue.
   - ❏ b. have long been an issue in industrial countries.
   - ❏ c. are an issue in every country in the world.

8. It is likely that diseases such as cancer and asthma
   - ❏ a. are caused solely by hazardous work environments.
   - ❏ b. can be eliminated in the workplace.
   - ❏ c. can be reduced if work environments are made less hazardous.

9. You can conclude from the article that businesses and industries
   - ❏ a. are not required to provide a healthy work environment.
   - ❏ b. are held responsible for work-related health problems.
   - ❏ c. feel no responsibility toward their workers' health.

10. Workers in countries that have little industry are probably
    - ❏ a. more likely to have work-related health problems.
    - ❏ b. less likely to have work-related health problems.
    - ❏ c. very healthy.

Rosie O'Dell sat at her workbench, one in a long row of women and girls. She swirled her paintbrush against her tongue to make a point on the brush's end and then dipped it into a pot of radium paint. She carefully painted a tiny number 2. Hour after hour she painted lines and numbers on dials to create watches that glowed in the dark.

Plant managers at U.S. Radium Corporation where Rosie worked told their workers that the radium paint was not only harmless, it was good for them. The dial painters did seem to take on a healthy glow—their hair, faces, hands, and arms shone. At night Rosie gazed into a mirror in a dark room and admired her glowing features.

In 1924, though, a dentist named Theodore Blum noticed that a patient who worked at U.S. Radium had a severe jaw infection. He wrote an article for the *Journal of the American Dental Association* in which he stated that he thought the infection was caused by a radioactive substance. When more dial painters developed cancer of the jaw, U.S. Radium claimed it was because of poor dental hygiene. However, when dial painters with bone diseases sued the company in 1927, it settled out of court.

1. **Recognizing Words in Context**

   Find the word *severe* in the passage. One definition below is a *synonym* for that word; it means the same or almost the same thing. One definition is an *antonym;* it has the opposite or nearly opposite meaning. The other has a completely different meaning. Label the definitions S for *synonym*, A for *antonym*, and D for *different*.

   _____ a. extreme

   _____ b. cruel

   _____ c. mild

2. **Distinguishing Fact from Opinion**

   Two of the statements below present *facts*, which can be proved correct. The other statement is an *opinion*, which expresses someone's thoughts or beliefs. Label the statements F for *fact* and O for *opinion*.

   _____ a. U.S. Radium should have been put out of business.

   _____ b. Dial painters at U.S. Radium developed cancer of the jaw.

   _____ c. U.S. Radium settled out of court when it was sued by dial painters.

3. Keeping Events in Order

Label the statements below 1, 2, and 3 to show the order in which the events happened.

_____ a. Rosie dipped her brush into a pot of radium paint.

_____ b. Rosie swirled a paintbrush on her tongue to make a point.

_____ c. Rosie painted a number on a watch dial.

4. Making Correct Inferences

Two of the statements below are correct *inferences,* or reasonable guesses. They are based on information in the passage. The other statement is an incorrect, or faulty, inference. Label the statements C for *correct* inference and F for *faulty* inference.

_____ a. The radium paint caused the workers' bone diseases.

_____ b. U.S. Radium believed that poor dental hygiene was the cause of its workers' cancer.

_____ c. The dial painters were not aware of the dangers of exposure to radiation from radium.

5. Understanding Main Ideas

One of the statements below expresses the main idea of the passage. One statement is too general, or too broad. The other explains only part of the passage; it is too narrow. Label the statements M for *main idea,* B for *too broad,* and N for *too narrow.*

_____ a. Radium, a highly radioactive substance discovered in 1898, was used to make paint that glowed in the dark.

_____ b. Rosie painted lines and numbers on watch dials with radium paint.

_____ c. Workers who painted watch dials with radium paint developed cancer of the jaw.

Correct Answers, Part A _____

Correct Answers, Part B _____

Total Correct Answers _____

19 | A | Lobbying

Attempts to influence the decisions of government are called lobbying. The term originated because attempts to put pressure on legislators often took place in the vestibule, or lobby, adjacent to the legislative chamber. The activity is most commonly associated with private interest groups, such as representatives of corporations or labor unions, but it may also be carried out by individuals. Legislators themselves, when they try to influence the making of public policy by other officials, are lobbyists.

In the United States, as well as in other popular democracies, the idea of representative government suggests that elected officials owe service to the people who live in their districts and states. Throughout the nineteenth and much of the twentieth centuries, however, elected officials were often controlled by private interests whose power and money could, among other things, aid in a political campaign. Thus, in the second half of the nineteenth century, during a period of rapid industrialization, representatives and senators passed a great deal of legislation favorable to the railroads, steel companies, oil companies, and other industries. These laws were frequently against the best interests of the public.

The power of industry over elected officials became so great that, in 1906, an investigative reporter named David Graham Phillips published a series of articles in which he exposed in detail the alliance between big business and the most influential senators. His articles, combined with a general public outrage over government scandals, led to a movement for reform in campaign financing. Beginning in 1907, a series of laws was passed, culminating in the 1925 Federal Corrupt Practices Act. Unfortunately, the laws were written in such a manner that their intent could easily be evaded.

In 1913, the ratification of the Seventeenth Amendment provided for the direct election of United States senators. Until then, they had been elected by the state legislatures and were, therefore, less accountable to the public than to the interests that helped them get elected. This amendment helped bring the Senate's work more into the spotlight and weaken the strong ties between business interests and the senators.

Demands to curb the excessive influence of pressure groups led to the Federal Regulation of Lobbying Act in 1946. The law requires lobbyists to register and report contributions and expenditures. The groups they represent must make similar reports. The assumption behind the law is that lobbyists cannot do much harm if their activities are publicized.

Reading Time _____

Recalling Facts

1. Lobbying refers to
   - ❑ a. attempts to influence the decisions of government.
   - ❑ b. activities that occur in vestibules.
   - ❑ c. activities of private interest groups.

2. David Graham Phillips
   - ❑ a. lobbied for steel companies.
   - ❑ b. exposed alliances between big business and senators.
   - ❑ c. wrote new laws controlling the power of industry.

3. The Seventeenth Amendment provided for
   - ❑ a. freedom of speech.
   - ❑ b. the regulation of lobbying.
   - ❑ c. the direct election of United States senators.

4. Lobbyists are required to
   - ❑ a. report contributions and expenditures.
   - ❑ b. finance presidential campaigns.
   - ❑ c. avoid talking to senators.

5. In a democracy, elected officials
   - ❑ a. owe service to the people.
   - ❑ b. should serve the interests of private industry.
   - ❑ c. are controlled by government standards.

Understanding Ideas

6. You can conclude from the article that before the Federal Regulation of Lobbying Act,
   - ❑ a. lobbying was illegal.
   - ❑ b. senators were appointed to office.
   - ❑ c. government scandals were common.

7. The article suggests that lobbyists are
   - ❑ a. honorable.
   - ❑ b. influential.
   - ❑ c. depraved.

8. Lobbying influenced senators through
   - ❑ a. threats and intimidation.
   - ❑ b. campaign contributions.
   - ❑ c. rapid industrialization.

9. The article suggests that the 1925 Federal Corrupt Practices Act
   - ❑ a. ended corrupt government practices.
   - ❑ b. increased government corruption.
   - ❑ c. had little effect on government corruption.

10. You can conclude from the article that the interests of the public and private industry are
    - ❑ a. usually the same.
    - ❑ b. often at odds.
    - ❑ c. determined by legislation.

"Senator! Senator! Just a moment!" The cry goes up from a group of waiting lobbyists as a senator strides toward his office.

"Senator, if I could talk to you about. . . ."

"Senator, about the upcoming vote. . . ."

"Senator, have you decided what. . ."

The senator ignores the lobbyists. He quickly opens his office door, enters, and closes it behind him. He greets his secretary with a grimace, and the secretary smiles understandingly. Then the senator enters the inner office and sighs as he relaxes into his leather chair.

In the past, the senator would have invited in one of the lobbyists and listened to his or her speech. He would have let the lobbyist buy him dinner at one of Washington's finest restaurants. He would have accepted a donation to his campaign fund. It would have been understood that his vote on some issue would favor that lobbyist.

Times had changed. The Federal Regulation of Lobbying Act made the activities of lobbyists public. And the public had not liked what it learned. People were angry that votes could bought and sold. The senator was up for reelection next year. The people in his home state would be very interested in where his campaign funds came from. No, the lobbyists would stay on the other side of the door today.

1. **Recognizing Words in Context**

Find the word *finest* in the passage. One definition below is a *synonym* for that word; it means the same or almost the same thing. One definition is an *antonym*; it has the opposite or nearly opposite meaning. The other has a completely different meaning. Label the definitions S for *synonym*, A for *antonym*, and D for *different*.

_____ a. most fine-grained

_____ b. worst

_____ c. best

2. **Distinguishing Fact from Opinion**

Two of the statements below present *facts*, which can be proved correct. The other statement is an *opinion*, which expresses someone's thoughts or beliefs. Label the statements F for *fact* and O for *opinion*.

_____ a. Lobbyists tried to get the senator's attention.

_____ b. The senator ignored the lobbyists.

_____ c. The senator was very rude.

3. Keeping Events in Order

Two of the statements below describe events that happened at the same time. The other statement describes an event that happened before or after those events. Label them S for *same time*, B for *before*, and A for *after*.

_____ a. Lobbyists called out to the senator.

_____ b. The senator sat in the leather chair in his office.

_____ c. The senator walked toward his office.

4. Making Correct Inferences

Two of the statements below are correct *inferences*, or reasonable guesses. They are based on information in the passage. The other statement is an incorrect, or faulty, inference. Label the statements C for *correct* inference and F for *faulty* inference.

_____ a. All lobbyists make campaign contributions to buy legislators' votes.

_____ b. The senator ignored the lobbyists because people in his home state did not approve of lobbying.

_____ c. The lobbyists wanted to influence the way the senator voted on certain issues.

5. Understanding Main Ideas

One of the statements below expresses the main idea of the passage. One statement is too general, or too broad. The other explains only part of the passage; it is too narrow. Label the statements M for *main idea*, B for *too broad*, and N for *too narrow*.

_____ a. Waiting lobbyists called out to get the attention of a senator.

_____ b. The term *lobbying* refers to attempts to influence the decisions of legislators.

_____ c. Because of concerns about the attitudes of people in his home state, a senator refuses to listen to lobbyists.

Correct Answers, Part A _____

Correct Answers, Part B _____

Total Correct Answers _____

20 | A | What Is Hypnosis?

Such an extraordinary phenomenon is hypnosis that no completely satisfactory definition has ever been developed. In fact, debates still rage over its exact nature. The British Medical Association and the American Medical Association have tentatively defined it as "a temporary condition of altered attention in the subject that may be induced by another person," but there is still much about hypnosis to be understood. Although the condition resembles normal sleep, scientists have found that the brain wave patterns of hypnotized subjects are much closer to the patterns of deep relaxation. Thus, rather than a psychic or mystical phenomenon, hypnosis is now generally viewed as a form of attentive, receptive, highly focused concentration in which external or peripheral events are omitted or disregarded.

The remarkable and characteristic feature of the hypnotic trance is that hypnotized persons become highly suggestible, or easily influenced by the suggestions or instructions of others—generally the hypnotist. They retain their powers to act and are able to walk, talk, speak, and respond to questions. Their perceptions, however, can be radically altered or distorted by external suggestions. At the command of the hypnotist, subjects may lose all feeling in a limb, and a pinprick will cause them no pain. They can be made to experience visual or auditory hallucinations or to regress in mental age and live the past as if it were the present. Subjects may forget part or all of the hypnotic experience or be made to recall things that they had otherwise forgotten.

The hypnotist may also make certain "posthypnotic suggestions"—instructions to the hypnotized subject to respond to a specified signal later, after awakening. For instance, the hypnotist might suggest that, at some time after the hypnotic session, the subject will resume the hypnotic state on signal. Such suggestions are sometimes used by certain medical specialists to repress or suggest away such symptoms in a patient as anxiety, itching, or headaches.

The suggestion that they are asleep and the fact that they have previously agreed to cooperate with the hypnotist make the subjects less critical than they would be if normally awake. In this state, they will accept commands and suggestions, even if the suggestions are illogical. In general, however, subjects cannot be made to follow instructions that conflict violently with their moral sense. For instance, subjects would not be likely to commit murder or robbery if directly instructed to do so.

Reading Time _____

Recalling Facts

1. The brain wave patterns of hypnotized subjects resemble those of
   - ❏ a. deep sleep.
   - ❏ b. light sleep.
   - ❏ c. deep relaxation.

2. A hypnotized subject seems
   - ❏ a. unaware of external events.
   - ❏ b. aware only of external events.
   - ❏ c. in control of external events.

3. A hypnotized subject is easily influenced by
   - ❏ a. changes in temperature.
   - ❏ b. the instructions of others.
   - ❏ c. visual stimulation.

4. Posthypnotic suggestions are instructions
   - ❏ a. given to the subject before the hypnotic session.
   - ❏ b. given to the subject after the hypnotic session.
   - ❏ c. for the hypnotized subject to follow after awakening.

5. Hypnotized subjects generally cannot be made to follow instructions that
   - ❏ a. are illogical.
   - ❏ b. conflict violently with their moral sense.
   - ❏ c. are given during a session.

Understanding Ideas

6. The phenomenon of hypnosis
   - ❏ a. is an unsolvable mystery.
   - ❏ b. is still not fully understood.
   - ❏ c. cannot be defined.

7. You can conclude from the article that hypnosis
   - ❏ a. can be a useful medical tool.
   - ❏ b. is merely a psychic phenomenon.
   - ❏ c. is considered illegal.

8. A potential danger of hypnosis is
   - ❏ a. the hypnotist's control over a subject.
   - ❏ b. its negative effect on the hypnotist.
   - ❏ c. a subject's inability to eat.

9. It is assumed that subjects being hypnotized
   - ❏ a. are doing so against their will.
   - ❏ b. have agreed to the procedure.
   - ❏ c. have severe problems.

10. You can conclude from the article that hypnosis
   - ❏ a. can be practiced on anyone.
   - ❏ b. should be part of every medical examination.
   - ❏ c. should be a carefully monitored procedure.

20　B　　A Mesmerizing Experience

Franz Anton Mesmer, an Austrian physician, was one of the first to treat patients by hypnosis. However, Dr. Mesmer was not aware of what was behind his medical successes. He believed that they were the result of a method he had developed in which he stroked patients with magnets.

Mesmer introduced his new method of "animal magnetism" to Paris in 1778. Many famous French people—including Queen Marie Antoinette—attended Mesmer's sessions.

Mesmer's patients were taken to a dimly lit room. Clothed in flowing, brightly colored robes, Mesmer entered the room waving a magic wand. He arranged his patients in a circle and had them join hands. Soft music played in the background as Mesmer moved from person to person. He fixed his eyes on each one, touching the person and speaking quietly in his hypnotic voice. Mesmer thought he was calling on supernatural forces to cure his patients. In reality, it was his own powers of suggestion—not magnetism and not the supernatural—that helped them.

Many reputable physicians supported Mesmer's claims. However, King Louis XVI appointed a scientific commission to investigate him. The investigators' report labeled Mesmer as a fraud. He fell into disfavor and died in obscurity in Switzerland in 1815.

1. **Recognizing Words in Context**

   Find the word *fixed* in the passage. One definition below is a *synonym* for that word; it means the same or almost the same thing. One definition is an *antonym;* it has the opposite or nearly opposite meaning. The other has a completely different meaning. Label the definitions S for *synonym,* A for *antonym,* and D for *different.*

   _____ a. directed

   _____ b. repaired

   _____ c. withdrew

2. **Distinguishing Fact from Opinion**

   Two of the statements below present *facts,* which can be proved correct. The other statement is an *opinion,* which expresses someone's thoughts or beliefs. Label the statements F for *fact* and O for *opinion.*

   _____ a. Franz Anton Mesmer treated patients by hypnosis.

   _____ b. Mesmer was a fraud.

   _____ c. Mesmer called his treatment method "animal magnetism."

3. **Keeping Events in Order**

Two of the statements below describe events that happened at the same time. The other statement describes an event that happened before or after those events. Label them S for *same time*, B for *before*, and A for *after*.

_____ a. Mesmer's patients joined hands in a circle.

_____ b. Mesmer fixed his eyes on a person.

_____ c. Mesmer spoke to and touched each patient.

4. **Making Correct Inferences**

Two of the statements below are correct *inferences*, or reasonable guesses. They are based on information in the passage. The other statement is an incorrect, or faulty, inference. Label the statements C for *correct* inference and F for *faulty* inference.

_____ a. Mesmer achieved some cures with his method.

_____ b. Hypnotism can be used to cure any illness.

_____ c. Because of the commission's findings, people no longer believed in Mesmer's ability.

5. **Understanding Main Ideas**

One of the statements below expresses the main idea of the passage. One statement is too general, or too broad. The other explains only part of the passage; it is too narrow. Label the statements M for *main idea*, B for *too broad*, and N for *too narrow*.

_____ a. Mesmer stroked his patients with magnets.

_____ b. Hypnosis is used by many therapists to treat anxiety, illnesses caused by stress, and addictions such as smoking.

_____ c. Franz Anton Mesmer, an Austrian physician, was one of the first to treat patients by hypnosis.

Correct Answers, Part A _____

Correct Answers, Part B _____

Total Correct Answers _____

A Chinese medical technique, acupuncture has been practiced for more than 4,000 years. It is used primarily for the relief of pain but also for curing disease and improving general health. Acupuncture consists of inserting hair-thin needles through particular spots in the skin. The acupuncture points are then stimulated by gentle twirling, by heat, or by stimulation with a weak electrical current. They also can be stimulated by pressure, ultrasound, and certain wavelengths of light.

Acupuncture appears to be effective in relieving pain. Western observers have witnessed ordinarily painful surgical operations carried out on fully conscious Chinese patients who were locally anesthetized only by acupuncture and exhibited no signs of discomfort. The reasons for acupuncture's success, however, are not understood. One theory suggests that the needle insertions stimulate the body's production of natural pain-killing chemical substances. Another theory suggests that acupuncture blocks the transmission of pain impulses from parts of the body to the central nervous system.

Acupuncture is still regarded legally in the United States as an experimental medical procedure. It has been used extensively in research projects in hospitals and medical centers throughout Asia, Europe, and North and South America. Acupuncture has been shown to relieve pain during and after dental procedures and in some surgical operations. It has also been used to control blood pressure and to relieve muscle spasms and arthritic pain. It has been used to alleviate symptoms associated with withdrawal from drug addiction, with appetite control, and with many other conditions. In some people and in certain medical conditions, it is not always effective. At one time, it was believed that acupuncture was related in some way to hypnosis, but extensive experiments with animals undergoing surgery in veterinary hospitals have disproved that assumption.

It has been difficult for modern physicians to accept acupuncture as an effective procedure for the treatment of certain conditions. This is primarily because of the elaborate systems of fanciful theories that were developed thousands of years ago by the early practitioners of acupuncture to explain its mechanisms of action.

In 1972, acupuncture received great publicity, particularly in the United States, as an indirect result of President Richard M. Nixon's trip to China. A newspaper correspondent who had accompanied Nixon reported on the pain relief provided by acupuncture after his emergency appendectomy. Since then, many United States physicians and dentists have been trained to administer acupuncture in courses authorized by state governments.

Reading Time _____

Recalling Facts

1. Acupuncture is used primarily for
   - ❏ a. curing disease.
   - ❏ b. relieving pain.
   - ❏ c. drug addiction.

2. Acupuncture involves
   - ❏ a. pinching the skin.
   - ❏ b. inserting thin needles into the skin.
   - ❏ c. skin grafts.

3. One theory of how acupuncture works is that
   - ❏ a. it blocks the transmission of pain impulses.
   - ❏ b. the patients are hypnotized.
   - ❏ c. it stimulates the body's electricity.

4. In the United States, acupuncture is regarded legally as
   - ❏ a. a miracle cure.
   - ❏ b. surgery.
   - ❏ c. an experimental medical procedure.

5. Acupuncture gained greater credibility in the United States following
   - ❏ a. President Nixon's trip to China.
   - ❏ b. World War II.
   - ❏ c. the introduction of acupuncture courses.

Understanding Ideas

6. Acupuncture points can be stimulated
   - ❏ a. only by a trained physician.
   - ❏ b. by a variety of methods.
   - ❏ c. primarily by electricity.

7. The United States has probably been reluctant to accept acupuncture treatment because
   - ❏ a. Chinese medicine is thought to be ineffective.
   - ❏ b. acupuncture is not clearly understood.
   - ❏ c. it is too expensive.

8. A major advantage of acupuncture used in surgical procedures is that
   - ❏ a. time is reduced.
   - ❏ b. surgery is always successful.
   - ❏ c. no anesthesia is necessary.

9. You can conclude from the article that acupuncture
   - ❏ a. is universally effective.
   - ❏ b. can cure most diseases.
   - ❏ c. is not for everyone.

10. It is likely that acupuncture treatment in the United States will probably
    - ❏ a. gain greater acceptance.
    - ❏ b. become less acceptable.
    - ❏ c. prove to be a hoax.

Junior, an elderly German shepherd, was in constant pain from arthritis in his hips and knees. He had trouble getting up, and he limped badly. When his vet could no longer help, she sent Junior and his owners to a veterinarian trained in acupuncture. Veterinary acupuncture is still relatively rare, but it is being used more often these days to treat animals like Junior, and it is proving effective.

Several years ago, a research scientist wanted to prove that acupuncture didn't really stop pain. He believed that acupuncture worked mostly on the mind, reducing pain only if people believed it would. For his experiments, therefore, he used animals. To his surprise, animals treated with acupuncture registered little or no response to pain. Researchers later discovered that acupuncture causes the brain to release chemicals called endorphins that block pain in animals as well as humans.

Junior's acupuncture veterinarian immobilizes him by having someone hold him or by giving him a mild drug. Then he inserts acupuncture needles at key points. In the beginning, Junior is treated once a week for eight weeks; later, about once a month.

Now Junior no longer limps. "He's like a young dog again," his owner says.

1. **Recognizing Words in Context**

Find the word *immobilizes* in the passage. One definition below is a *synonym* for that word; it means the same or almost the same thing. One definition is an *antonym*; it has the opposite or nearly opposite meaning. The other has a completely different meaning. Label the definitions S for *synonym*, A for *antonym*, and D for *different*.

_____ a. moves around

_____ b. holds motionless

_____ c. examines

2. **Distinguishing Fact from Opinion**

Two of the statements below present *facts*, which can be proved correct. The other statement is an *opinion*, which expresses someone's thoughts or beliefs. Label the statements F for *fact* and O for *opinion*.

_____ a. Junior's vet sent him to a veterinary acupuncturist.

_____ b. Acupuncture causes the brain to release pain-blocking chemicals.

_____ c. Junior acts like a young dog again.

3. **Keeping Events in Order**

Label the statements below 1, 2, and 3 to show the order in which the events happened.

_____ a. Junior was limping badly from arthritis.

_____ b. Junior received acupuncture treatments.

_____ c. Junior no longer limps.

4. **Making Correct Inferences**

Two of the statements below are correct *inferences*, or reasonable guesses. They are based on information in the passage. The other statement is an incorrect, or faulty, inference. Label the statements C for *correct* inference and F for *faulty* inference.

_____ a. Acupuncture does help block pain.

_____ b. Acupuncture works mainly because people think it will.

_____ c. Acupuncture is an effective way to treat pain in animals.

5. **Understanding Main Ideas**

One of the statements below expresses the main idea of the passage. One statement is too general, or too broad. The other explains only part of the passage; it is too narrow. Label the statements M for *main idea*, B for *too broad*, and N for *too narrow*.

_____ a. Acupuncture has different uses.

_____ b. The veterinarian treats the pet with acupuncture once a week by inserting needles at key points.

_____ c. Veterinarians are now using acupuncture to treat animals for pain.

Correct Answers, Part A _____

Correct Answers, Part B _____

Total Correct Answers _____

22 | A | Letter Writing

A direct, written message that is usually sent some distance from one person to another or to a group of people or an organization is called a letter. Over time, letter writing has also developed into a popular literary prose form, a type of biographical or autobiographical literature, intended in some cases for reading by the general public.

Letter writing began in the ancient world as soon as rulers of nations, separated by distance, found the need to communicate with each other. It is known from a collection of documents found in Egypt that many rulers in the ancient Middle East kept up a lively correspondence with the pharaohs. Among the ancients, Cicero was a prolific writer of letters, especially to his friend Atticus. In the Bible, most of the books in the New Testament are letters from St. Paul and other Christian leaders to various congregations and individuals. Throughout history, many well-known persons have written letters that, although originally intended as private correspondence, have been collected and published. Such collections are far too numerous to list. For example, in the modern period, the letters of such famous people as Charles Lamb, Robert Louis Stevenson, William Dean Howells, Ernest Hemingway, Groucho Marx, Sigmund Freud, Woodrow Wilson, George Eliot, Henry James, Virginia Woolf, Katherine Mansfield, and D.H. Lawrence have been rich sources of information on the people themselves and on the world as they saw it. In the matter of published letters, it should be noted that a letter as a document becomes the property of the recipient, but the contents remain the property of the sender, who must consent to any publication.

In the late twentieth century, the practice of letter writing has diminished considerably. This is probably due to the influence of mass communication technologies such as telephones and computers. Still, some types of personal correspondence remain in use: formal invitations and replies, business letters, thank-you notes and letters, and letters of application. Of these kinds of correspondence, only the thank-you note and letter are generally written at the warm, personal level. Invitations, for example, hardly seem to be letters at all, since they often are engraved on high-quality paper and are very formal. One kind of correspondence that is more public than personal is the letter to the editor, an individual expression of opinion on some issue of current interest written to be published in newspapers and magazines.

Reading Time _____

Recalling Facts

1. Letter writing satisfies the need for
   - ❏ a. communication between people.
   - ❏ b. setting down facts for history.
   - ❏ c. practicing penmanship.

2. Cicero wrote many letters to his friend
   - ❏ a. Caesar.
   - ❏ b. Atticus.
   - ❏ c. St. Paul.

3. Most of the books in the New Testament are
   - ❏ a. biographical essays.
   - ❏ b. sermons given by Christian leaders.
   - ❏ c. letters from Christian leaders to congregations and individuals.

4. The contents of a letter are the property of the
   - ❏ a. public.
   - ❏ b. sender.
   - ❏ c. recipient.

5. A letter to the editor of a newspaper
   - ❏ a. expresses the opinion of the sender.
   - ❏ b. is not intended for publication.
   - ❏ c. expresses the opinion of the newspaper.

Understanding Ideas

6. You can conclude from the article that most letters are intended
   - ❏ a. for publication.
   - ❏ b. as private correspondence.
   - ❏ c. for personal diaries.

7. It is likely that modern communication technology has
   - ❏ a. eliminated the need for writing letters.
   - ❏ b. encouraged the need for writing letters.
   - ❏ c. lessened the need for writing letters.

8. Personal letters published after the death of famous persons are valued because
   - ❏ a. they provide a personal point of view on people and events.
   - ❏ b. the writers wanted them to be made public.
   - ❏ c. privacy has been violated.

9. You can conclude from the article that publishing a letter without the consent of the sender is
   - ❏ a. a common practice.
   - ❏ b. against the law.
   - ❏ c. acceptable if the sender is famous.

10. The article suggests that personal correspondence has generally become
   - ❏ a. more personal.
   - ❏ b. less formal.
   - ❏ c. more formal.

22 B   A Trip to Forget

Dear Amanda,

You're not going to believe what happened on our train trip to Seattle to spend Thanksgiving with Gram and Gramp. It took 57 hours to get there from Chicago. We arrived 12 hours late. And all because Dad thought going by train would be an adventure. It was, but not the kind of adventure he had in mind.

First, police boarded the train in Wisconsin and took off one of the passengers. Next, the train hit a car that had been abandoned on the tracks. We had to wait about an hour and a half for the wreckage to be hauled away. Luckily, no one was hurt.

We'd finally gotten as far as Idaho when a freight train up the line derailed. We sat there, going nowhere, for eight hours while workers cleared the tracks. Some people held a sing-along to pass the time. The worst thing was that the dining car ran out of food! The train stopped in Spokane, Washington, to pick up more food. I think the crew was afraid we'd revolt if they didn't feed us.

I tell you, Amanda, I was never so thankful for anything in my life as getting off that train. A stagecoach might have been faster.

Your friend,
Lily

1. Recognizing Words in Context

Find the word *boarded* in the passage. One definition below is a *synonym* for that word; it means the same or almost the same thing. One definition is an *antonym;* it has the opposite or nearly opposite meaning. The other has a completely different meaning. Label the definitions S for *synonym,* A for *antonym,* and D for *different.*

_____ a. entered

_____ b. left

_____ c. covered

2. Distinguishing Fact from Opinion

Two of the statements below present *facts,* which can be proved correct. The other statement is an *opinion,* which expresses someone's thoughts or beliefs. Label the statements F for *fact* and O for *opinion.*

_____ a. The train hit a car that was abandoned on the tracks.

_____ b. A derailed freight train delayed the train eight hours.

_____ c. The worst thing was that the dining car ran out of food.

3. Keeping Events in Order

Two of the statements below describe events that happened at the same time. The other statement describes an event that happened before or after those events. Label them S for *same time*, B for *before*, and A for *after*.

_____ a. Crews cleared the derailed freight train from the tracks.

_____ b. The train sat there, going nowhere, for eight hours.

_____ c. The train arrived in Seattle 12 hours late.

4. Making Correct Inferences

Two of the statements below are correct *inferences*, or reasonable guesses. They are based on information in the passage. The other statement is an incorrect, or faulty, inference. Label the statements C for *correct* inference and F for *faulty* inference.

_____ a. It is unusual for so many bad things to happen during a single train trip.

_____ b. The train trip from Chicago to Seattle normally takes far less than 57 hours.

_____ c. Every train trip is an adventure.

5. Understanding Main Ideas

One of the statements below expresses the main idea of the passage. One statement is too general, or too broad. The other explains only part of the passage; it is too narrow. Label the statements M for *main idea*, B for *too broad*, and N for *too narrow*.

_____ a. Misadventures that happened on a train trip from Chicago to Seattle delayed the train's arrival for 12 hours.

_____ b. Crews took eight hours to clear a derailed freight train from the tracks.

_____ c. Taking a train trip can prove to be an adventure.

Correct Answers, Part A _____

Correct Answers, Part B _____

Total Correct Answers _____

23 | A | Aborigine

From prehistoric times to the present, there have been many mass migrations of people throughout the world. In a few isolated locations, however, certain tribal or ethnic groups have lived without migrating for many thousands of years. Such people are called aborigines, from Latin, meaning "from the beginning." Aboriginal peoples lived in areas remote from other cultures, and their existence became known to the rest of the world only when outsiders intruded upon their territories.

Some anthropologists in the twentieth century question whether aborigines have always lived in the locations where they have been found in modern times. It is possible that some aborigines did migrate, but in a period so remote in time that there is no record of their migration. In the case of the Indians of the Americas, for instance, it is generally accepted that their ancestors came to the Western Hemisphere by way of the Bering Strait between Siberia and Alaska many thousands of years ago.

In the twentieth century, there are few regions of the world where outsiders have not encroached upon aboriginal cultures. Stone Age cultures exist in the jungles of South America and on the island of New Guinea. The Negritos, a pygmylike people of Malaysia and the Philippines, live in the mountainous interiors and have succeeded in preserving their primitive ways of life without much interference.

On Hokkaido, the large northern island of Japan, live a people called the Ainu, who were originally distinct physically from the surrounding Mongoloid population. Over the centuries, the processes of cultural assimilation and intermarriage have almost eliminated their distinctive characteristics. They now resemble the Japanese in appearance and use the Japanese language.

By virtue of their name, the Australian aboriginals (or aborigines, as they are also called) are probably the best known of the aboriginal societies. At the time of the first European settlement about 200 years ago, the aboriginals occupied all of Australia and the island of Tasmania. The estimate of the eighteenth-century population was at least 300,000, comprising more than 500 tribes.

Most anthropologists and archaeologists believe that the aboriginals migrated to Australia and Tasmania about 40,000 years ago. They probably originated in mainland Southeast Asia and may have reached Australia by way of a now-submerged land shelf that connected the continent with New Guinea. Since the arrival of European settlers in Australia, the traditional aboriginal way of life has been adversely affected.

Reading Time _____

Recalling Facts

1. The name *aborigine* comes from Latin meaning
   - ❏ a. "from the beginning."
   - ❏ b. "prehistoric times."
   - ❏ c. "migrating people."

2. Aborigines are people who have
   - ❏ a. recently moved to an area.
   - ❏ b. migrated frequently from place to place.
   - ❏ c. lived in one place for thousands of years.

3. The Ainu of Japan are an example of
   - ❏ a. people who have retained distinctive characteristics.
   - ❏ b. cultural assimilation and intermarriage.
   - ❏ c. an untouched primitive aboriginal culture.

4. Aboriginal cultures exist
   - ❏ a. around the world.
   - ❏ b. primarily in the East.
   - ❏ c. where rainfall is frequent.

5. The ancestors of some aborigines migrated from continent to continent by traveling
   - ❏ a. in boats.
   - ❏ b. on sleds.
   - ❏ c. over now-submerged land.

Understanding Ideas

6. The effect of outsiders on aboriginal cultures has been
   - ❏ a. positive.
   - ❏ b. negative.
   - ❏ c. neutral.

7. Some aboriginal cultures have remained unaffected by outsiders because
   - ❏ a. the aborigines are too primitive.
   - ❏ b. the aborigines live in very remote areas.
   - ❏ c. outsiders have no interest in meeting them.

8. The article suggests that nonmigrating peoples tend to
   - ❏ a. retain their distinct characteristics.
   - ❏ b. mix with other cultures.
   - ❏ c. lose their traditions.

9. Since the 1900s, the aboriginal population in Australia has
   - ❏ a. increased.
   - ❏ b. decreased.
   - ❏ c. remained the same.

10. The Indians of the Americas are considered
    - ❏ a. assimilated cultures.
    - ❏ b. Stone Age cultures.
    - ❏ c. aboriginal cultures.

The aborigines of Australia tell tales about the beginning of their people. Long ago, they say, in a time called the Dreaming or Dreamtime, their ancestors wandered the earth, which was flat and featureless. As the ancestors wandered, they sang, scattering musical notes and words along their path. As they sang, the mountains and the creeks and all the other features of the land appeared, created by their songs.

After the land came to be, the ancestors made humans and animals out of clay and sang life into them. The people that the ancestors made became the aboriginal people of Australia.

Long after those first beings vanished, their songs remained. Each geographical feature, every hill and water hole and rock, every streambed had its own story, its own sacred beginning, and, most importantly, its own song. The paths between the features are known as songlines. The aborigines did not have maps or charts or writing, and when they wanted to explain how to go from one place to another, they did not explain in words. Instead, they sang.

Today, an aboriginal person will often commence a long journey into wild places he or she has never been, taking no map and following no roads—just following the ancestors' songlines.

1. **Recognizing Words in Context**

    Find the word *commence* in the passage. One definition below is a *synonym* for that word; it means the same or almost the same thing. One definition is an *antonym;* it has the opposite or nearly opposite meaning. The other has a completely different meaning. Label the definitions S for *synonym,* A for *antonym,* and D for *different.*

    _____ a. begin

    _____ b. end

    _____ c. talk about

2. **Distinguishing Fact from Opinion**

    Two of the statements below present *facts,* which can be proved correct. The other statement is an *opinion,* which expresses someone's thoughts or beliefs. Label the statements F for *fact* and O for *opinion.*

    _____ a. Aboriginal people tell stories of their beginnings.

    _____ b. Aboriginal people often journey into wild places.

    _____ c. Aboriginal people prefer following songlines to following maps.

3. Keeping Events in Order

Label the statements below 1, 2, and 3 to show the order in which the events happened.

_____ a. Aboriginal ancestors wandered the earth, singing.

_____ b. The ancestors created Australia's animals and people.

_____ c. The aborigines tell stories about their beginnings.

4. Making Correct Inferences

Two of the statements below are correct *inferences*, or reasonable guesses. They are based on information in the passage. The other statement is an incorrect, or faulty, inference. Label the statements C for *correct* inference and F for *faulty* inference.

_____ a. Aboriginal people have a strong traditional culture.

_____ b. Aboriginal people keep their traditions alive.

_____ c. Aborigines are no longer interested in their background.

5. Understanding Main Ideas

One of the statements below expresses the main idea of the passage. One statement is too general, or too broad. The other explains only part of the passage; it is too narrow. Label the statements M for *main idea*, B for *too broad*, and N for *too narrow*.

_____ a. Australia was created long ago.

_____ b. Australia's geographical features came from the songs of aboriginal people.

_____ c. According to Australian aborigine belief, their ancestors created the world through song.

Correct Answers, Part A _____

Correct Answers, Part B _____

Total Correct Answers _____

24 | A | Calling All Engineers

The building of canals, bridges, and roads was carried out by specially trained civil engineers as early as the middle of the eighteenth century. With the advent of steam power at the beginning of the Industrial Revolution in the last part of the eighteenth century, mechanical engineers started to develop engines, locomotives, and various other machines. Originally, steam was used merely to extend power beyond that of animals. During the nineteenth century, however, mechanical engineering expanded to include such laborsaving devices as the sewing machine and the mechanical reaper.

The increasing need for metals furthered mining engineering. With the invention of the Bessemer steel-making process, steel began to replace iron in both machinery and construction. Large bridges and skyscrapers became possible. This led to the development of metallurgical engineering as a separate field. The invention of electric generators and motors and the development of the electric light bulb led to the growth of electrical engineering. This was originally a subspecialty of mechanical engineering. Advances in chemistry during the latter half of the nineteenth century demanded that small-scale laboratories be expanded to large-scale production. This opened the way for the chemical engineer. All these various fields of engineering had been established by 1900.

Following the introduction of the assembly line by Henry Ford, the demands of the growing automobile industry led to a specialty in automotive engineering. The rapid spurt of airplane development following World War I led to the new field of aeronautical engineering. The increasing need for petroleum products to provide fuels for transportation, energy generation, and heating fostered petroleum engineering. With the development of radio just after the turn of the twentieth century, electronic engineering was born. Radio, television, and almost all modern communications techniques depend on the electronic engineer. Following the invention of the transistor, new vistas in communications and computing were opened. The information revolution caused by the computer added computer engineering as a new specialty.

The advent of nuclear power was reflected in the field of nuclear engineering. Combinations of medicine and technology to build artificial limbs or organs and to improve medical instrumentation started the field of bioengineering.

The need to produce goods cheaply and efficiently became a primary responsibility of the industrial engineer. Following the development of space flight, aerospace engineering was added to aeronautical engineering. A number of further specialty areas also came about such as ceramic, safety, agricultural, environmental, and transportation engineering.

Reading Time _____

Recalling Facts

1. Steam power was introduced at the beginning of
   - ❏ a. the Industrial Revolution.
   - ❏ b. World War II.
   - ❏ c. the Revolutionary War.

2. Iron in machinery and construction was replaced by
   - ❏ a. aluminum.
   - ❏ b. ceramics.
   - ❏ c. steel.

3. Electronic engineering was fostered by the development of
   - ❏ a. the sewing machine.
   - ❏ b. the radio.
   - ❏ c. television.

4. Among other things, bioengineering involves building
   - ❏ a. nuclear power stations.
   - ❏ b. airplanes.
   - ❏ c. artificial limbs and organs.

5. Industrial engineers are concerned with
   - ❏ a. improving medical instrumentation.
   - ❏ b. producing goods cheaply and efficiently.
   - ❏ c. developing new areas of communication.

Understanding Ideas

6. You can conclude from the article that engineering
   - ❏ a. is a broad field with many specialty areas.
   - ❏ b. is restricted to industrial applications.
   - ❏ c. specializes in aeronautical applications.

7. Engineers are concerned with
   - ❏ a. the practical applications of science.
   - ❏ b. the aesthetics of science.
   - ❏ c. literary achievement.

8. Specialty areas in engineering developed as a result of
   - ❏ a. production demands.
   - ❏ b. advances in science and technology.
   - ❏ c. global conflicts.

9. Engineers are likely to be
   - ❏ a. methodical.
   - ❏ b. artistic.
   - ❏ c. disorganized.

10. You can conclude from the article that the field of engineering
    - ❏ a. is becoming too specialized.
    - ❏ b. is limited in the number of specialty areas that can be developed.
    - ❏ c. will probably continue to develop more specialty areas.

Engineering a Change

Henry Rowan stood in the melting room of the Philadelphia mint. The owner of Inductotherm, a small company that manufactured melting furnaces, he had made an outrageous claim. He could, he had said, change the melting units in the mint's furnaces in just ten minutes—a job that the mint foreman claimed took four hours. Moreover, Rowan had bragged, he would change the units with the furnaces loaded with metal and heated to 3,000 degrees.

Rowan had begun his engineering career with a company that built melt systems—furnaces that heated metal until it became liquid. He soon started Inductotherm with a few good workers and very little cash. Winning the mint's contract was essential if his fledgling company were to survive.

Rowan disconnected the cables from the old furnaces and began to connect the new ones. The first three connections went smoothly. The last one refused to catch. Finally, Rowan felt the cable tighten. Cold water poured into the furnace, preventing a meltdown. Rowan had succeeded.

Henry Rowan went on to build Inductotherm into a hugely successful business. In 1995, he donated $100,000,000 to a small college in New Jersey for an engineering school that now bears his name: Rowan College.

1. Recognizing Words in Context

Find the word *fledgling* in the passage. One definition below is a *synonym* for that word; it means the same or almost the same thing. One definition is an *antonym*; it has the opposite or nearly opposite meaning. The other has a completely different meaning. Label the definitions S for *synonym*, A for *antonym*, and D for *different*.

_____ a. young bird

_____ b. established

_____ c. new

2. Distinguishing Fact from Opinion

Two of the statements below present *facts*, which can be proved correct. The other statement is an *opinion*, which expresses someone's thoughts or beliefs. Label the statements F for *fact* and O for *opinion*.

_____ a. Rowan's claim was outrageous.

_____ b. Rowan founded Inductotherm.

_____ c. Rowan gave $100,000,000 to a college in New Jersey.

3. Keeping Events in Order

Label the statements below 1, 2, and 3 to show the order in which the events happened.

_____ a. Inductotherm became hugely successful.

_____ b. Rowan worked for a company that built melt systems.

_____ c. Rowan founded his own company.

4. Making Correct Inferences

Two of the statements below are correct *inferences,* or reasonable guesses. They are based on information in the passage. The other statement is an incorrect, or faulty, inference. Label the statements C for *correct* inference and F for *faulty* inference.

_____ a. Engineering can be an exciting field.

_____ b. Henry Rowan was a risk taker.

_____ c. Changing melting units is a simple task.

5. Understanding Main Ideas

One of the statements below expresses the main idea of the passage. One statement is too general, or too broad. The other explains only part of the passage; it is too narrow. Label the statements M for *main idea,* B for *too broad,* and N for *too narrow.*

_____ a. Henry Rowan, whose gift created Rowan College, won business for his young company through a daring demonstration.

_____ b. Henry Rowan took risks to get his company started.

_____ c. Henry Rowan began his engineering career with a company that built furnaces and then founded a company of his own.

Correct Answers, Part A _____

Correct Answers, Part B _____

Total Correct Answers _____

Atmospheric conditions, particularly variations in the weather and their effects on the Earth, are the subject of meteorology. This science uses physics and chemistry to unravel the dynamics of the Earth's atmosphere in an attempt to understand, predict, and control atmospheric actions.

The sun is the engine that drives the Earth's weather. Due to the uneven heating of the Earth's surface, the atmosphere is in a constant state of imbalance, or disequilibrium. Weather conditions are a result of the atmosphere's attempt to gain equilibrium—a state it never achieves. This constant struggle for equilibrium combines with the influence of the Earth's rotation and the gravitational pulls of the sun and moon to keep the atmosphere in constant motion. Large masses of air move and mix, rise and sink, absorb and release energy to produce the vast panorama of atmospheric conditions that we commonly refer to as the weather.

Both meteorology and climatology are particular sciences concerned with the study and prediction of weather conditions. Meteorology deals with the specific weather conditions at a given time and place. Climatology is concerned with average weather conditions over extended periods of time and in areas all over the globe.

Synoptic and dynamic meteorology are two major branches of meteorology. Synoptic meteorologists use simultaneous weather reports to analyze the present state of the atmosphere and predict its future states. Dynamic meteorologists use mathematical equations to describe the motions of the atmosphere. Because the atmosphere behaves according to the laws of physics, dynamic meteorologists can use computers to solve equations and predict the future state of the atmosphere—a technique called numerical weather prediction (NWP). Synoptic meteorologists routinely modify these numerical weather predictions to account for the effects of local conditions and landforms such as large bodies of water, deserts, and mountains.

Virtually every segment of society benefits from weather forecasts: the aviation, maritime, and energy industries; potable-water-management and pollution-control agencies; agricultural organizations; defense departments; and, of course, the general public. Moreover, accurate weather forecasts are becoming increasingly important. Thus, most governments, many universities, and some private corporations sponsor meteorological research programs that range from investigations of the atmosphere to improved methods for modifying weather predictions. Modern research programs emphasize the numerical modeling of such local conditions as thunderstorms and heavy rainfall, and researchers are developing computer models that will provide forecasts of weather conditions as many as ten to thirty days in advance.

Reading Time _____

Recalling Facts

1. The Earth's atmosphere is in a state of imbalance due to
   - ❏ a. poor weather forecasts.
   - ❏ b. uneven heating of the Earth's surface.
   - ❏ c. moisture absorption.

2. The science that deals with extended global weather conditions is called
   - ❏ a. meteorology.
   - ❏ b. atmospherics.
   - ❏ c. climatology.

3. Scientists who use mathematical equations to describe the motions of the Earth's atmosphere are
   - ❏ a. dynamic meteorologists.
   - ❏ b. synoptic meteorologists.
   - ❏ c. synoptic climatologists.

4. NWP stands for
   - ❏ a. new wave precipitation.
   - ❏ b. national weather program.
   - ❏ c. numerical weather prediction.

5. The atmosphere behaves according to the laws of
   - ❏ a. technology.
   - ❏ b. physics.
   - ❏ c. mathematics.

Understanding Ideas

6. The article suggests that weather prediction is important to
   - ❏ a. most segments of society.
   - ❏ b. only a small part of society.
   - ❏ c. every single person on Earth.

7. The atmosphere will probably
   - ❏ a. eventually achieve a state of equilibrium.
   - ❏ b. remain in a constant state of imbalance.
   - ❏ c. vacillate between imbalance and equilibrium.

8. The article wants you to understand that weather prediction is
   - ❏ a. largely guesswork.
   - ❏ b. based on scientific principles.
   - ❏ c. usually inaccurate.

9. You can conclude from the article that scientists are able to
   - ❏ a. change the weather.
   - ❏ b. control weather patterns under certain conditions.
   - ❏ c. predict how local conditions will affect the future state of the atmosphere.

10. The article suggests that the prediction of weather conditions well in advance is
    - ❏ a. likely to happen.
    - ❏ b. unlikely to happen.
    - ❏ c. impractical.

In 1897, Charles Dudley Warner wrote, "Everybody talks about the weather, but nobody does anything about it." But in the late 1940s, people trained as meteorologists during World War II began to reenter the peacetime workforce, bringing their skills with them.

Another new technology was spreading in the 1940s—television. News programs began hiring weather forecasters. The first forecasters worked on a shoestring. They drew weather patterns on charts with chalk or used stick-on symbols. Some early forecasters were actors, not scientists. In 1959, the American Meteorological Society began certifying TV forecasters, thereby raising professional standards.

In 1955, viewers experienced radar images of weather for the first time as television tracked Hurricane Diane. In the early 1960s, a few stations began broadcasting images from the first weather satellites. By the 1970s, most stations featured satellite pictures, and people could see actual weather patterns for themselves.

In 1982, the Weather Channel, with its sophisticated computer graphics, was born. Today anyone can tune in to a scientifically accurate weather forecast for anywhere in the world, 24 hours a day. The National Weather Service relies heavily on television to disseminate information to the public about dangerous weather conditions. Televised weather warnings help save many lives each year.

1. **Recognizing Words in Context**

   Find the word *tracked* in the passage. One definition below is a *synonym* for that word; it means the same or almost the same thing. One definition is an *antonym*; it has the opposite or nearly opposite meaning. The other has a completely different meaning. Label the definitions S for *synonym*, A for *antonym*, and D for *different*.

   _____ a. avoided

   _____ b. followed

   _____ c. traveled

2. **Distinguishing Fact from Opinion**

   Two of the statements below present *facts*, which can be proved correct. The other statement is an *opinion*, which expresses someone's thoughts or beliefs. Label the statements F for *fact* and O for *opinion*.

   _____ a. Everybody talks about the weather, but nobody does anything about it.

   _____ b. Television tracked Hurricane Diane with radar in 1955.

   _____ c. The Weather Channel began in 1982.

3. Keeping Events in Order

Two of the statements below describe events that happened at the same time. The other statement describes an event that happened before or after those events. Label them S for *same time*, B for *before*, and A for *after*.

_____ a. Television viewers saw radar images of Hurricane Diane.

_____ b. People trained as meteorologists entered the workforce.

_____ c. Television was becoming widespread.

4. Making Correct Inferences

Two of the statements below are correct *inferences*, or reasonable guesses. They are based on information in the passage. The other statement is an incorrect, or faulty, inference. Label the statements C for *correct* inference and F for *faulty* inference.

_____ a. Knowing about approaching dangerous weather conditions is not particularly helpful.

_____ b. Television helped popularize the science of meteorology.

_____ c. The National Weather Service and television work well together.

5. Understanding Main Ideas

One of the statements below expresses the main idea of the passage. One statement is too general, or too broad. The other explains only part of the passage; it is too narrow. Label the statements M for *main idea*, B for *too broad*, and N for *too narrow*.

_____ a. Meteorology, new to most people in the 1940s, became a popular science through television weather forecasts.

_____ b. The history of television weather forecasts began in the 1940s.

_____ c. Today anyone can get a scientifically accurate weather forecast for anywhere in the world, 24 hours a day.

Correct Answers, Part A _____

Correct Answers, Part B _____

Total Correct Answers _____

ANSWER KEY

READING RATE GRAPH

COMPREHENSION SCORE GRAPH

COMPREHENSION SKILLS PROFILE GRAPH

ANSWER KEY

1A	1. b	2. c	3. b	4. b	5. a	6. c	7. b	8. a	9. a	10. b
1B	1. D, A, S	2. F, O, F	3. 1, 3, 2	4. C, C, F	5. M, N, B					
2A	1. a	2. b	3. c	4. b	5. a	6. c	7. a	8. b	9. c	10. b
2B	1. D, A, S	2. F, O, F	3. 2, 1, 3	4. F, C, C	5. M, B, N					
3A	1. b	2. b	3. a	4. c	5. c	6. a	7. a	8. a	9. b	10. b
3B	1. S, A, D	2. F, O, F	3. S, B, S	4. C, C, F	5. B, M, N					
4A	1. b	2. a	3. b	4. c	5. a	6. b	7. c	8. b	9. c	10. a
4B	1. A, S, D	2. F, F, O	3. 1, 2, 3	4. C, F, C	5. B, N, M					
5A	1. c	2. a	3. b	4. c	5. a	6. a	7. c	8. b	9. a	10. b
5B	1. S, A, D	2. F, O, F	3. 2, 1, 3	4. C, C, F	5. M, N, B					
6A	1. b	2. b	3. a	4. b	5. c	6. b	7. a	8. b	9. c	10. b
6B	1. A, S, D	2. F, F, O	3. 2, 3, 1	4. C, F, C	5. B, N, M					
7A	1. a	2. c	3. b	4. a	5. b	6. b	7. c	8. a	9. b	10. a
7B	1. D, S, A	2. O, F, F	3. 2, 3, 1	4. C, F, C	5. N, M, B					
8A	1. b	2. a	3. a	4. b	5. c	6. a	7. c	8. b	9. c	10. b
8B	1. A, S, D	2. F, F, O	3. 1, 2, 3	4. C, F, C	5. B, N, M					
9A	1. c	2. b	3. b	4. a	5. c	6. c	7. a	8. b	9. c	10. a
9B	1. S, D, A	2. F, O, F	3. 3, 1, 2	4. C, F, C	5. N, B, M					
10A	1. a	2. b	3. a	4. c	5. b	6. a	7. b	8. c	9. b	10. c
10B	1. D, S, A	2. F, O, F	3. S, S, A	4. F, C, C	5. N, M, B					
11A	1. c	2. b	3. a	4. c	5. a	6. b	7. a	8. c	9. b	10. a
11B	1. S, A, D	2. O, F, F	3. S, A, S	4. F, C, C	5. M, B, N					
12A	1. c	2. b	3. a	4. a	5. c	6. b	7. a	8. b	9. c	10. a
12B	1. A, D, S	2. O, F, F	3. S, A, S	4. F, C, C	5. M, B, N					
13A	1. b	2. a	3. b	4. c	5. b	6. a	7. c	8. a	9. c	10. a
13B	1. S, A, D	2. F, F, O	3. 2, 1, 3	4. C, F, C	5. B, N, M					

14A	1. b	2. c	3. c	4. a	5. b	6. a	7. b	8. c	9. b	10. a
14B	1. A, S, D		2. F, F, O		3. 1, 2, 3		4. C, F, C		5. B, N, M	
15A	1. a	2. b	3. c	4. b	5. a	6. a	7. b	8. c	9. a	10. b
15B	1. S, D, A		2. F, F, O		3. S, S, A		4. C, C, F		5. N, B, M	
16A	1. a	2. a	3. c	4. b	5. b	6. a	7. c	8. a	9. b	10. c
16B	1. S, D, A		2. F, O, F		3. 2, 3, 1		4. C, C, F		5. N, B, M	
17A	1. c	2. a	3. b	4. b	5. a	6. b	7. a	8. a	9. c	10. c
17B	1. A, S, D		2. O, F, F		3. 3, 2, 1		4. F, C, C		5. M, N, B	
18A	1. a	2. c	3. c	4. a	5. a	6. c	7. b	8. c	9. b	10. b
18B	1. S, D, A		2. O, F, F		3. 2, 1, 3		4. C, F, C		5. B, N, M	
19A	1. a	2. b	3. c	4. a	5. a	6. c	7. b	8. b	9. c	10. b
19B	1. D, A, S		2. F, F, O		3. S, A, S		4. F, C, C		5. N, B, M	
20A	1. c	2. a	3. b	4. c	5. b	6. b	7. a	8. a	9. b	10. c
20B	1. S, D, A		2. F, O, F		3. B, S, S		4. C, F, C		5. N, B, M	
21A	1. b	2. b	3. a	4. c	5. a	6. b	7. b	8. c	9. c	10. a
21B	1. A, S, D		2. F, F, O		3. 1, 2, 3		4. C, F, C		5. B, N, M	
22A	1. a	2. b	3. c	4. b	5. a	6. b	7. c	8. a	9. b	10. c
22B	1. S, A, D		2. F, F, O		3. S, S, A		4. C, C, F		5. M, N, B	
23A	1. a	2. c	3. b	4. a	5. c	6. b	7. b	8. a	9. b	10. c
23B	1. S, A, D		2. F, F, O		3. 1, 2, 3		4. C, C, F		5. B, N, M	
24A	1. a	2. c	3. b	4. c	5. b	6. a	7. a	8. b	9. a	10. c
24B	1. D, A, S		2. O, F, F		3. 3, 1, 2		4. C, C, F		5. M, B, N	
25A	1. b	2. c	3. a	4. c	5. b	6. a	7. b	8. b	9. c	10. a
25B	1. A, S, D		2. O, F, F		3. A, S, S		4. F, C, C		5. M, B, N	

READING RATE

Put an X on the line above each lesson number to show your reading time and words-per-minute rate for that unit.

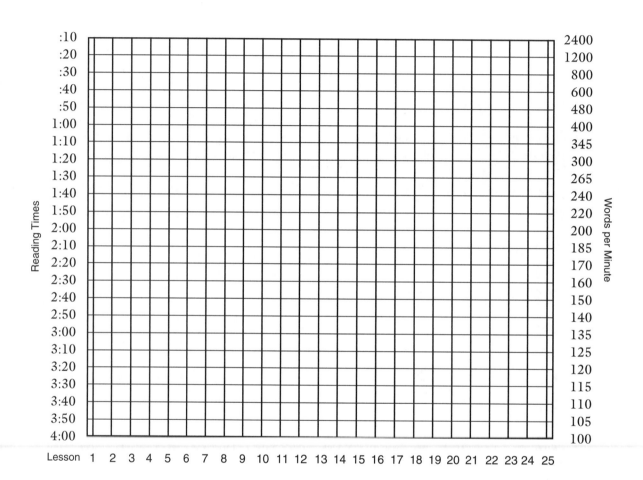

COMPREHENSION SCORE

Put an X on the line above each lesson number to indicate your total correct answers and comprehension score for that unit.

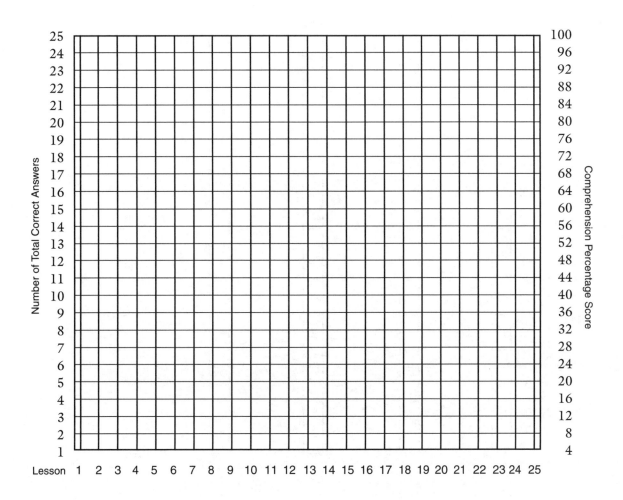

COMPREHENSION SKILLS PROFILE

Put an X in the box above each question type to indicate an incorrect reponse to any part of that question.

Lesson	Recognizing Words in Context	Distinguishing Fact from Opinion	Keeping Events in Order	Making Correct Inferences	Understanding Main Ideas
1					
2					
3					
4					
5					
6					
7					
8					
9					
10					
11					
12					
13					
14					
15					
16					
17					
18					
19					
20					
21					
22					
23					
24					
25					